# GUNPOWDER

## ABOUT THE AUTHOR

Harneet Baweja and his wife Devina Seth grew up in Kolkata, and from an early age food played an important role in both their families as they enjoyed recipes that had been passed down for generations. They moved to London in 2014 and set up Gunpowder restaurant with head chef Nirmal Save. Nirmal is originally from Mumbai, where he grew up on a farm and developed a keen interest in the ingredients and produce his mother and grandmother taught him to cook.

www.gunpowderlondon.com   Instagram: @gunpowder_london   Twitter: @gunpowder_ldn

# GUNPOWDER

## EXPLOSIVE FLAVORS
## FROM MODERN INDIA

HARNEET BAWEJA,
DEVINA SETH, AND NIRMAL SAVE

Photography by Peter Cassidy

KYLE BOOKS

# TO MOTHERS AND
# GRANDMOTHERS

Published in 2018 by Kyle Books
www.kylebooks.com

Distributed by National Book Network
4501 Forbes Blvd, Suite 200,
Lanham, MD 20706
Phone: (800) 462-6420
Fax: (800) 338-4550
customercare@nbnbooks.com

First published in Great Britain in 2018
by Kyle Cathie Limited
Part of Octopus Publishing Group Limited

ISBN 978-1-909487-86-4

The publishers would like to thank
Rachel de Thample for her contribution

Project Editor: Tara O'Sullivan
Copy Editor: Vicki Murrell
Editorial Assistant: Sarah Kyle
Designer: Evi O. / Evi O. Studio
Typesetting: Jo Wright and Susan Le / Evi O. Studio
Photographer: Peter Cassidy*
Illustrator: Our Place
Food Stylist: Aya Nishimura
Prop Stylist: Iris Bromet
Production: Nic Jones and Gemma John
*see page 192 for additional photo credits

Library of Congress Control Number: 2018931952

Printed in China

10 9 8 7 6 5 4 3 2 1

# INTRODUCTION

Indian food is a vast treasure trove. It is a unique collection of multiple cultures and centuries-old recipes handed down and personalized by every household. My wife Devina, Head Chef Nirmal Save and I have carefully collected the gems and jewels of our family's kitchen secrets to create Gunpowder, a homestyle Indian kitchen restaurant. Now, we have gathered them into this book to share with you.

## OUR INDIAN STORY

Growing up in Kolkata, I was surrounded by the mingling flavors and aromas of my family's cooking and the city's street food. School days were rounded off with waiting in line for *pani puri*, an enormously popular snack of hollow *puri*, fried until crisp and filled with tamarind chutney, chaat masala, potato or chickpeas—delicious flavors that we enjoyed together, standing or sitting with family and friends. Then we would rush home to Maa's Kashmiri lamb chops. These beautifully spiced chops remain one of my favorite foods, and you can find the recipe on page 00.

Devina is also from Kolkata and our lives very much interlinked around the Indian foods of the city. Her mother and grandmother cooked delectable meals that they created and adapted in their own ways. Devina undertook an education and career away from the kitchen but even with a degree in journalism and a Masters from Goldsmiths, the craving for the cuisine of Kolkata never faded for her, such as fond memories of her favorite comfort food *kichdi*—a mix of rice and lentils which her granny made for her growing up.

Kolkata is a cultural and intellectual hub, buzzing with Ambassador taxis whizzing past, swarms of people going about their daily lives, and the ever popular hum of street food vendors offering piping hot delicacies. The city has an abundance of market stands and food stalls such as Dacres Lane, where my wife and I have whiled away hours trying every creation you can think of, from traditional Bengali *ghugni* (dried white peas mixed with tamarind, chiles, and jaggery) to Bengali's own take on Chinese chow mein, which uses turmeric and chicken masala for a twist on the original.

Originally from Mumbai, Nirmal was born into a family of second-generation farmers. He began cooking alongside his mother and grandmother at just 12 years old. They introduced him to a variety of regional dishes and flavors and passed on their closely guarded recipes. Growing up on the farm ensured he was surrounded by fresh produce, spending his hours catching game, digging up vegetables, and collecting fruit from the Sapodilla trees, thus instilling in him a lifelong appreciation for cooking with fresh ingredients.

## OUR LONDON STORY

Devina and I moved to London in 2014. We were instantly captivated by the city, and its vibrant and diverse restaurant scene. What was striking, however, was that despite knowing how much the English love their curries, we felt they were missing out on a huge part of what makes Indian food so special: the intricacy of flavors found in home-style dishes. We couldn't find anything like this on the market.

Thus, we sought to create a restaurant centerd around incredible family recipes passed down from generation to generation, learnt at our mothers' feet. We all grew up surrounded by this and we've missed it since moving to London.

## OUR RESTAURANT STORY

We opened Gunpowder, a home-style Indian kitchen, in 2015 at White's Row, Spitalfields. Taking residence in an old curry house, the restaurant is named after the spice mix "gunpowder", a heady blend of pulses and spices, including chile, curry leaves and *hing*, Hindi for asafoetida.

It's a happy coincidence that we are located close to Brick Lane, so famous for its curries, though it feels to us as if it has lost its soul. We wanted to bring something new and fresh to the scene, adding to the changing face of British curry, and bringing to it a sense of experimentation mixed with family tradition.

Since we opened, we have been delighted to find our 20-cover restaurant full at every lunch and dinner time, with people sometimes queuing in the street for a table. For us, the essence of Gunpowder is the smell of savory spices mingling and the sound of friends laughing and talking as they gather to share plates of the food of our childhood.

# SPICE GLOSSARY

**ASAFOETIDA**
Extracted from a plant of the giant fennel family, asafoetida is known for having a pungent smell but, by contrast, it adds a subtle flavor to dishes when cooked with other spices. It's a brilliant alternative to garlic and onions in dishes.

**BLACK CARDAMOM**
The pods of black cardamom are larger than the more-familiar green variety and they have a smoky character derived from the method of drying over open flames.

**BLACK CUMIN (NIGELLA) SEEDS**
Also known as nigella, black cumin is one the most revered medicinal seeds in history and it's one of the oldest spices known to be used. The tiny black seeds have a slightly bitter taste with some of the pungency of onion but also offer many other subtle nuances of flavor.

**BLACK HORSE GRAMS**
These small flattened lentils, multi-colored in a spectrum that goes from beige to dark coffee brown, are one of the most protein-rich pulses on the planet. Historically, race horses were fed with this gram, hence its name.

**BOONDI**
These water droplet-sized, deep-fried crispy Indian snacks are made with chickpea flour and few spices. It's a main ingredient in making boondi raita and other snacks.

**CAROM SEEDS**
The use of carom seeds is mostly limited to India, in particular, Gujarat. The seeds have a thyme-like flavor and are traditionally used in roti and paratha.

**CHAAT MASALA**
Chaat is a generic name for hot, tangy, sweet nibbles but here it refers to a zingy, tangy, slightly hot spice blend. It gets its distinctive flavor from the black salt used to make it. Though often used as a spice in cooking, chaat masala is mostly used as a garnish on salads.

**CHANA MASALA**
This is a special blend of spices used to make a traditional chickpea curry. While every household will have their own unique recipe, many recipes feature asafoetida, nutmeg, ginger, cardamom, mango powder, cumin, fennel, black pepper, cloves, chile, cinnamon, bay, and fenugreek.

**CLUSTER BEANS**
The guar or cluster bean is a very valuable plant. Agriculturists in semi-arid regions of Rajasthan follow crop-rotation and grow these beans not only as a source of food, but also to replenish the soil before the next crop. In dishes, the beans offer a distinct flavor with a slightly bitter taste which works well with spices and rich sauces.

**CURRY LEAVES**
A staple of South Indian cooking, curry leaves are used in Indian and South East Asian cuisine in the same way as bay leaves are used in the West. The shiny, dark green, aromatic leaves are harvested from a tree in the citrus family. When fried in hot oil, curry leaves release a deliciously nutty aroma.

**DEGGI MIRCH**
Deggi mirch is a full-flavored Indian spice that's milder than chile powder but hotter than paprika. You can buy it in Indian grocers or online. Or, to make an easy substitute, mix 2 tablespoons paprika with 1 tablespoon chile powder.

**DRIED POMEGRANATE SEEDS**
Also known as anardana, dried pomegranate seeds are sold in Indian as commonly as you would find sun-dried raisins or cranberries in the West. The seeds are often powdered to add a tangy, sour, and sweet flavor to dishes and spice blends.

**FENUGREEK**
Both fenugreek leaves and seeds, known as methi in Hindi, are important ingredients in Indian cooking. They offer a subtle yet notable flavor that's somewhat like a cross between liquorice and fennel. Fenugreek is also hailed in ayurvedic medicine for its digestive and antioxidant benefits.

**GARAM MASALA**
The word garam refers to 'heating the body' in the Ayurvedic sense of the word. While the composition of garam masala differs regionally across the Indian subcontinent, each blend is believed to elevate body temperature.

**GHEE**
Ghee is a class of clarified butter that originated from the Indian subcontinent. It was historically made with butter made from water buffalo milk. Today, cow's milk butter is commonly used. As it's heated for longer, ghee has a stronger, nuttier flavor, and darker color than standard clarified butter. Its higher burning point means that it's good for frying.

## GUNPOWDER SPICE
Gunpowder is a traditional South Indian dry condiment made from roasted lentils, sesame seeds, curry leaves, and other spices. It's traditionally used as a seasoning for idlis, rice or noodles.

## JAGGERY
Jaggery is a completely unrefined sugar made from sugar cane juice or palm sap that is cooked down and set into blocks.

## KASHMIR CHILES
With a vibrant red hue and very delicate heat, the Kashmiri chiles are used as much for their color enriching properties as they are for their subtle, fruity chile notes. Heat-wise, they're on the same level as Mexican poblano chiles.

## KHUS
Khus is a dark green thick syrup made from the roots of khus grass (vetiver grass). It has a grassy, woody flavor that's often compared with that of lemongrass.

## MADRAS CURRY POWDER
This is an aromatic blend of spices, often with a fair bit of heat, which is typical of the Madras region. The curry blend often features roasted and ground coriander, mustard, turmeric, black chickpeas, cumin, fenugreek, black pepper, garlic, fennel, and salt.

## MANGO GINGER
Also known as curcuma amada, mango ginger is a plant of the ginger family and is closely related to turmeric. It's traditionally used in pickles and chutneys.

## MANGO POWDER
This is a fruity spice powder made from dried unripe green mangoes and is used as a citrusy seasoning. Also known as amchoor, it has a distinctive citrusy taste not too dissimilar to sumac, and is prized for offering the nutritional benefits of mangoes when the fresh fruit is out of season. It's a staple in many Indian spice blends.

## MUSTARD OIL
This oil has a distinct mustard flavor and is the traditionally preferred oil for cooking in North and Eastern India.

## NAGA CHILES
This is one of the hottest chile peppers ever measured. It was briefly the 'World's Hottest Chile' in 2011 according to the Guinness World Records with a rating of 1,382,118 Scoville units.

## STONE FLOWER
Also known as black stone flower, this is a soft, dark lichen that gives the signature black hue to various masalas. It has a woody aroma and imparts a strong earthy flavor when cooked. It is widely used in Chettinad cuisine and, to some extent, in Hyderabadi and Marathi cuisines.

## TAMARIND
Tamarind is a leguminous tree producing pod-like fruits containing an edible pulp with a distinct sweet and tangy flavor.

## URAD DAL
Urad dal, also called urid dal, is made from hulled and split urad beans. This pale-yellow pulse doesn't require pre-soaking and is valued for its nutty flavor and creamy texture. It's the key ingredient used to make poppadoms, as well as as idli (steamed urad dal and rice cakes), dosa (thin, crisp-textured rice and lentil pancakes), and uttapam (sourdough pancakes).

## YELLOW CHILE POWDER
Compared to the fiery red chiles, yellow chiles are mild and mostly used to enhance the color of dishes, as well as imparting a more subtle flavor. The yellow variety of chile used to make this distinctive powder is mainly grown in Punjab and South Kashmir.

## YELLOW MOONG
Yellow moong dal refers to moong beans that have been skinned and split, so that they're flat, yellow, and quick-cooking.

## NOTE
Everyone has different tastes, so if you are sensitive to chile or other spices, feel free to tweak and adjust the quantities in our recipes to suit your palate.

# SMALL
# PLATES

# SMALL PLATES

When I was a child, my mother always had things in the refrigerator she could feed us for a snack or base a meal around. The following dishes are inspired by this. They are the nucleus of family food. The Chickpea Pancakes (see page 17) are a great example. You can make a large batch of batter, fry up some pancakes for breakfast and store the remaining mixture in the refrigerator so that you can whip up fresh hot pancakes on a whim. The Kale and Corn Cakes (see page 18) are another classic. We eat them for breakfast at home, but they make a great snack, or you can serve them with rice or even as a vegetarian burger.

You can also treat these dishes as Indian tapas or mezze of sorts, which, of course, is how we serve them in the restaurant. Enjoy our small plates as you wish and make them connect with your home and way of life.

# SALLI PAR EEDU

SERVES 4

Parsees migrated from Greater Iran to Sindh and Gujarat, where they were given refuge, between the eighth and tenth centuries to avoid persecution following the Arab conquest of Persia. This migration brought the influence of Persian food to the local cuisine, this dish being a perfect example. It's like an Indian take on shakshuka.

4 cups sunflower or canola oil, for frying
4 potatoes, peeled and julienned
3 tablespoons ghee
4 tomatoes, finely chopped
½ teaspoon freshly ground black pepper, plus extra to taste
½ teaspoon garam masala (store-bought, or see page 161)
5 tablespoons freshly chopped cilantro
4 eggs
bread, to serve
sea salt

1 Heat the oil in a skillet over high heat until it's sputtering, then deep fry the julienned potatoes in small batches (about 1 handful for each batch), until the sticks are crisp and golden. Remove with a slotted spoon and drain on paper towels then sprinkle with a little salt and let sit.

2 Heat the ghee in a large skillet with a lid. Add the chopped tomatoes, ½ teaspoon black pepper, the garam masala and a pinch of salt, and cook for about 10 minutes until the tomatoes have broken down and thickened to a sauce. Add the fried potato sticks and spread out to cover the base of the skillet, pressing down gently with a spatula to create a thick layer.

3 Fold in half the chopped cilantro, then make four little nests in the potato mix and crack an egg into each nest. Season the eggs with salt and pepper and cover with the lid.

4 Cook on low heat for about 10 minutes until the eggs whites are fully set and the yolk is still runny. Scatter with the remaining cilantro and serve immediately with your choice of bread.

## NOTE

For a lighter dish, instead of deep-frying, toss the julienned potatoes with 2 tablespoons oil and roast in an oven preheated to 400°F for 40 minutes or until golden.

# CHICKPEA PANCAKES

MAKES 12

This is one of my father's go-to breakfasts, which he'd happily eat every day. He likes the pancakes with chopped cilantro, red onion and green chile, but there are so many variations. Nirmal serves them with freshly grated coconut, or you can drizzle them with honey and serve with fruit. Alternatively, go savory and match with fried eggs and one of the chutneys at the back of the book (see pages 184–186).

1⅓ cup chickpea flour
⅔ cup all-purpose white flour
½ cup cornstarch
1 tablespoon soft brown sugar
½ teaspoon baking powder
½ teaspoon turmeric powder
⅔ cup natural yogurt
a pinch of sea salt
5 tablespoons freshly grated
   or dried coconut
1 thumb-sized piece of ginger,
   peeled and finely chopped
1 green chile, finely chopped
4–5 tablespoons butter or oil, for cooking

TO SERVE (OPTIONAL)
fried eggs
Tomato and cilantro Chutney (see
   page 186)

1 In a large bowl, combine the flours, cornstarch, brown sugar, baking powder, and turmeric. In another bowl, whisk the yogurt, salt, and ⅔ cup water together, then stir into the dry ingredients until the batter is smooth and the consistency of heavy cream.

2 Mix the coconut, ginger, and chile in a separate bowl and have at the ready.

3 Place a large skillet over medium heat. Add 1–2 teaspoons of butter or oil and, when hot, add a ladle (3–4 tablespoons) of batter and swirl the skillet to achieve a thin and even layer. Sprinkle a good pinch of the grated coconut mix over the surface of the pancake and cook for 2–3 minutes or until bubbles form on the top and the edges shrink from the sides of the skillet. Flip the pancakes and cook for an additional minute or until both sides are golden brown. Remove from the skillet and keep warm while you make the next pancake. Continue in this way until you've used up all the batter—you can freeze any surplus pancakes or batter for up to 6 months.

4 Serve warm with fried eggs and Tomato and cilantro Chutney, or the topping of your choice.

# KALE AND CORN CAKES

MAKES ABOUT 12 LITTLE CAKES

This is the sort of dish you'd find in school canteens back home in India. I used to love these as a kid. In fact, I still do. I love eating them with the spicy heat of mustard dolloped on the side. They also work well with ketchup or, as Nirmal suggests, a raita.

3 tablespoons canola or olive oil, plus extra for shallow frying
1 green chile, finely chopped
1 tablespoon freshly grated ginger
3½ ounces kale, washed, dried and finely chopped
½ cup fresh or canned sweetcorn kernels, drained
½ teaspoon smoked paprika
½ teaspoon garam masala (store-bought, or see page 161)
¼ teaspoon cumin seeds
7 ounces boiled potatoes, coarsely grated
½ cup panko breadcrumbs
4 tablespoons freshly chopped cilantro
sea salt, to taste
chutney or raita, to serve

1  Place a large non-stick skillet over high heat. Swirl the oil around the pan, then add the chile, ginger, and kale, and cook until the kale starts to wilt, about 5 minutes.

2  Fold in the sweetcorn and spices and cook for an additional 2–3 minutes, then take off the heat. Add the grated potato, Panko breadcrumbs, and fresh cilantro. Season with salt, to taste, and mix well until everything comes together. Let sit to cool.

3  Once cooled, divide the mixture into 12–15 golf ball-sized nuggets and roll each ball between your palms until smooth, then gently press to flatten a little into the shape of a disc.

4  Place the skillet back on high heat and add the oil for shallow-frying. When hot, cook the kale and corn cakes in small batches until golden on each side and then transfer to a paper towel-lined plate. Serve hot with any raita or tangy chutney.

# MARKET-STYLE SCRAMBLED EGGS

SERVES 4

In Indian markets, the vendors cook everything on smoking hot plates. The heat is so intense that you can't achieve that wonderful creamy texture you get when you scramble eggs over controlled heat at home. To get around this, they add onion and tomato, and, of course, lots of herbs and spices, which keeps the eggs moist and delicious. It's a true taste of Indian street food. I love these eggs for breakfast, but they're great anytime.

12 medium eggs
3 tablespoons ghee
6 curry leaves (fresh or dried)
1 teaspoon cumin seeds
½ teaspoon yellow mustard seed
1 onion, finely chopped
1 thumb-sized piece of ginger, peeled and finely chopped
1 green chile, finely chopped
2 tomatoes, finely chopped
1 ounce freshly chopped cilantro
1 tablespoon butter, plus extra to finish
1 teaspoon turmeric powder
a pinch of chile powder
a pinch of asafoetida (optional)
5 tablespoons finely chopped chives
grilled sourdough bread, to serve
sea salt

1 In a large bowl, whisk the eggs and let sit.

2 Set a large skillet over medium heat. Add the ghee and, once melted, add the curry leaves, cumin, mustard seeds, onion, ginger, and green chile. Sauté for 3–4 minutes. Add the tomatoes, fold through half the chopped cilantro, and cook for 2 minutes.

3 Add the butter, turmeric, chile powder, asafoetida (if using), and a good pinch of sea salt or more, to taste, and stir to mix well. Pour in the beaten eggs and keep whisking until they are cooked.

4 Add a little extra butter, if you like, and garnish with the remaining chopped cilantro leaves and chopped chives. Serve with grilled and buttered white sourdough bread.

# BEEF GUJIYA

MAKES 12–15

My father and a lot of men his age like to keep fit, so they go out in the morning for a long walk or run. However, once they've finished with all that exercise, they can't resist the temptation of tucking into one of these classic street food pastries. The classic preparation is to deep-fry them, and, of course, they're delicious that way. But if you're more health conscious, you can shallow fry or bake them instead and they'll still taste wonderful.

FOR THE PASTRY
14 ounces baby leaf spinach, washed
1 tablespoon fenugreek leaves or seeds,
   ground to a powder
6 tablespoons ghee
4 cups all-purpose flour
¾ cup fine semolina
3 teaspoons superfine sugar
1 teaspoon sea salt
6 tablespoons canola or olive oil
4 cups sunflower or canola oil, for frying

FOR THE FILLING
1 pound ground beef
3 tablespoons natural or Greek yogurt
1 teaspoon turmeric powder
4 garlic cloves, finely minced
1 teaspoon cumin seeds
seeds from 3 green cardamom pods
seeds from 1 black cardamom pod
4 cloves
½ cinnamon stick
6 black peppercorns
3 tablespoons canola or olive oil
2 onions, finely chopped
1 tablespoon freshly grated ginger
1 green chile, finely chopped
a pinch of chile powder
1 tablespoon ground coriander
1 large tomato, finely chopped
5 tablespoons freshly chopped cilantro

### FOR THE PASTRY

1 Place a skillet with a lid over high heat, add the spinach and fenugreek, and cover. Take off the heat immediately and let sit to let the spinach wilt down.

2 Transfer the wilted spinach into a strainer and squeeze to remove any excess liquid, then purée in a blender with 1 tablespoon of the ghee. Let sit.

3 Sift the flour into a bowl. Add the semolina, sugar, and salt, and stir to mix. Add the remaining ghee and oil and, using your fingers, mix well to incorporate so that the mixture takes the form of breadcrumbs and binds to a certain extent.

4 Add the spinach mixture and mix again with your hands, kneading lightly. If the dough is too dry, add 1–2 tablespoons water, just enough to bring it together into a soft but tight pastry dough. If it's too wet, add a little more flour. Let sit and cover with a damp cloth for 20 minutes.

### FOR THE FILLING

5 In a bowl, mix together the beef, yogurt, turmeric, and garlic, then let sit for 30 minutes–1 hour in the refrigerator.

6 Place a large skillet over medium heat. Add the cumin seeds, green and black cardamom seeds, cloves, cinnamon, and black peppercorns and toast for 1–2 minutes or until fragrant. Transfer to a coffee grinder or mortar and pestle and grind to a powder, then let sit.

7 Place the skillet back on the heat. Add the oil and, once hot, sauté the onions until golden. Stir in the ground spice mix, the ginger, green chile, chile powder, and ground coriander and cook for a minute, then fold in the tomatoes. Cook for 5–10 minutes or until the tomatoes have broken down into a thick paste.

8 Stir the marinated ground beef into the skillet and cook on medium heat for 15 minutes or until the mince is just golden. Fold the chopped cilantro through and let sit to cool slightly.

### TO ASSEMBLE THE PASTRIES

9 Divide the dough into 12–15 small balls and, using a rolling pin, roll out each ball into a 4-inch-diameter circle.

10 Fill half the circle with the filling mixture (about a tablespoon), leaving space around the edges, moisten the edges with water, then fold the pastry over and seal the filling in by curling the edges inwards, like a Cornish pasty. Take care that the filling does not ooze out. Prepare all the gujiyas in the same way and spread out on a clean dish towel.

11 Heat the oil in a deep skillet over high heat until it's sputtering. Lower the heat a little and deep-fry the pastries, in small batches, for about 5 minutes until golden. Make sure each pastry has plenty of space in the pan. Once cooked, transfer to a paper towel-lined tray. Serve immediately or gently warm further in an oven preheated to 350°F for 10 minutes.

## NOTE

Gujiya moulds can also be used—they are easily available. Place the rolled-out dough in a greased gujiya mould and add a tablespoon of filling mixture on one side. Moisten the edges and fold one side of the mould over the other. Trim the excess edges and reuse.

# ALOO GUJIYA

MAKES 12–15

This is the vegetarian spin on gujiya—and it's just as, if not more, delicious than its meaty counterpart (see page 22). The spinach gives the pastry a vibrant green hue.

**FOR THE PASTRY**
14 ounces baby leaf spinach, rinsed and drained
1 tablespoon fenugreek leaves or seeds, ground to a powder
6 tablespoons ghee
4 cups all-purpose flour, plus extra if needed
¾ cup fine semolina
2 teaspoons superfine sugar
1 teaspoon sea salt
5 tablespoons canola or olive oil
4 cups sunflower or canola oil, for frying

**FOR THE FILLING**
3 tablespoons canola or olive oil
2 bay leaves
1 teaspoon cumin seeds
2 large onions, finely chopped
3 tablespoons freshly grated ginger
2 garlic cloves, finely minced
½ teaspoon sea salt
1 teaspoon freshly ground black peppercorns
a pinch of chile powder
2 pounds new potatoes, boiled and skinned
3 tablespoons freshly squeezed lime juice
2 teaspoons ground cumin*
1 ounce cilantro leaves, finely chopped

**FOR THE PASTRY**
1  Place a skillet with a lid over high heat, add the spinach and fenugreek and cover. Take off the heat immediately and let sit to let the spinach wilt.

2  Transfer the wilted spinach into a strainer and squeeze to remove any excess liquid, then purée in a blender with 1 tablespoon of the ghee. Let sit.

3  Sift the flour into a bowl. Add the semolina, sugar, and salt, and stir to mix. Add the remaining ghee and the 5 tablespoons oil and, using your fingers, mix well to incorporate so that the mixture takes the form of breadcrumbs and binds to a certain extent.

4  Add the spinach mixture and mix again with your hands, kneading lightly. If the dough is too dry, add 1–2 tablespoons water, just enough to bring it together into a soft pastry dough. If it's too wet, add a little more flour. Let sit, covered with a damp cloth, for 20 minutes.

**FOR THE FILLING**
5  Place a pot over high heat. Add the oil, reduce the heat to medium, and add the bay leaves and cumin seeds. Wait for the cumin seeds to sputter, then fold in the onion, ginger, and garlic and gently fry for 10 minutes until the onions turn golden brown. Add the salt, black pepper, and chile powder and cook for 2–3 minutes until the oil separates from the mixture.

6  Place the potatoes into the pot and stir to coat in all the spices, crushing and mashing them as you mix them through. Add the lime juice and ½ cup water to moisten the mix and boil just enough so that the spice mixture is absorbed by the potatoes, but not so much that they break up.

7  Sprinkle with roasted cumin powder and the chopped cilantro leaves, then let sit to cool down. Once the mixture is cool, mash a little more to give you a smooth filling.

TIP

For maximum flavor, dry-roast whole cumin seeds for 1–2 minutes or until fragrant, and grind in a spice or coffee grinder or a mortar and pestle, to make your own roasted ground cumin. The difference in flavor compared to store-bought ground cumin is remarkable.

## TO ASSEMBLE THE PASTRIES

8 Divide the dough into 12–15 small balls and, using a rolling pin, roll out each ball of dough into a 4 inch-diameter circle.

9 Fill half the circle with the aloo mixture (about a tablespoon), leaving space around the edges. Moisten the edges of the pastry with a little water, then fold the pastry over and seal the filling in by curling the edges inwards, like a Cornish pasty. Take care that the filling does not ooze out. Prepare all the gujiyas in the same way and spread out on a clean dish towel.

10 Heat the oil in a deep skillet over high heat until it's sputtering. Reduce the heat a little and deep-fry the pastries, in small batches, for about 5 minutes until golden. Make sure each pastry has plenty of space in the skillet. Once cooked, transfer to a paper towel-lined tray. Serve immediately or gently warm further in an oven preheated to 350°F for 10 minutes.

### NOTE

Gujiya moulds can also be used – see note on page 23.

# LAMB KIDNEY AND CHICKEN LIVER ON TOAST

SERVES 4

This is another of my dad's best-loved dishes. In India, we waste nothing. Instead of buying just the chicken breast or thigh, we buy the whole chicken. The same thing applies to lamb—we don't want just the shank or the cutlet. It has to be sustainable and affordable at the same time. This means we have all the extras to use up and this is one of our favorite ways of cooking the livers and kidneys.

¼ cup canola oil or butter
2 onions, thinly sliced
4 garlic cloves, finely minced
8 curry leaves (fresh are best if you can get them, but dried are fine)
2 teaspoons garam masala (store-bought, or see page 161)
1 teaspoon turmeric powder
¼ teaspoon chile powder
4 cloves, finely ground
¼ cup tomato purée
½ pound trimmed chicken livers
½ pound cored lamb kidney
sea salt

TO SERVE
freshly chopped cilantro or micro herbs (such as radish or baby mustard leaves)
grilled sourdough bread

1 Heat the oil or butter in a large skillet over medium heat, add the onions and a pinch of salt, and cook for 5–10 minutes or until soft and a little golden.

2 Add the garlic and curry leaves and cook for 30 seconds, then stir in the garam masala, turmeric, chile powder, and cloves. Add the tomato purée and fry for about 5 minutes until oil is released and it turns brown.

3 Add the chicken livers and kidney and pour in 1 cup water. Stir well once, then cover and simmer over low heat for 10 minutes.

4 Remove the lid, stir again and check the thickness of the gravy, adding a little more water if needed. Season with salt, to taste, then serve on grilled sourdough with fresh cilantro or micro herbs scattered on top.

TIP

For best results, once cooked, leave to cool, then cover and refrigerate this dish for 6 hours or overnight, as then the liver and kidney absorb all the oil and masala flavor. Gently reheat, adding a little more water if necessary. Add extra curry leaves if you don't like the aroma/taste of fresh cooked liver and kidney.

# PORZI OKRA

This recipe has South Indian roots, where bindi or okra is very popular. This is the sort of thing Indian mothers make to get their children to eat green vegetables.

1 pound okra, cut into 4 lengthwise
1½ tablespoons freshly squeezed lemon juice
1 cup chickpea flour
1 tablespoon dry mango powder
1 tablespoon chile powder
½ teaspoon Gunpowder Spice Mix
  (see page 158)
20 curry leaves, (fresh are best if you can
  get them, but dried are fine), toasted and
  crushed to a powder
4 cups sunflower oil, for deep-frying
1 tablespoon chaat masala
sea salt

1 In a bowl, mix the okra with the lemon juice and let sit. In a separate large bowl, mix the chickpea flour with the dried mango powder, chile powder, gunpowder spice, and powdered curry leaves and a good pinch of salt. In small batches, coat the okra in the seasoned chickpea flour.

2 Pour the oil into a deep, heavy-bottomed pan suitable for deep-frying and set over high heat until sputtering. Check if the oil is hot enough by adding one piece of coated okra—it should rise to the top and crisp within 1–2 minutes.

3 When your oil is hot enough, fry the coated okra in small batches for 3 minutes until crisp and golden. Remove with a slotted spoon and drain on paper towels. Continue until all the okra is cooked, then serve immediately with a sprinkling of chaat masala and a dusting of salt on top.

# SAVORY
# FRENCH TOAST

SERVES 4

When I was little, we used to watch a lot of American TV programmes like *The Wonder Years*. We became so curious about American food through these shows. My mother created this dish to cater to our curiosity. Of course, she's given it an Indian twist.

3 eggs
¼ teaspoon turmeric powder
4 tablespoons milk
1 green chile, very finely chopped
½ teaspoon freshly grated ginger
1 garlic clove, finely minced
3 tablespoons freshly chopped cilantro
1 tablespoon finely chopped scallions
1 cherry tomato, finely chopped
4 thick slices of brioche, sliced on the
  diagonal
3–4 tablespoons butter, for cooking
sea salt and freshly ground black pepper
Tomato and Coriander Chutney (see page
  186), to serve

1 In a shallow dish, whisk the eggs with the turmeric and milk, then add the chile, ginger, garlic, cilantro, scallions, and tomato. Season with a good pinch of salt and black pepper.

2 Dip the bread in the egg mixture, one piece at a time, and let it soak for 15–30 seconds on each side, or until nicely coated. Let any excess mixture drip off the bread, then let sit.

3 Melt 1 tablespoon of the butter in a non-stick skillet set over medium heat and, in batches, fry each piece of eggy bread on both sides for 2–3 minutes until golden brown.

4 Work quickly and serve immediately with homemade Tomato and Coriander Chutney.

# MUSTARD BROCCOLI

# MAKHANI SAUCE

SERVES 2 AS A MAIN, 4 AS A STARTER OR SIDE

MAKES 1 CUP

We use mustard a lot in the east of India and here we pair it with broccoli, which is in the same family. In India, you often see this dish made with cauliflower, so you could easily interchange them. We prefer broccoli for the restaurant, as it really soaks in all the flavors and gets even crisper when flashed under the grill. It's one of the most popular vegetarian dishes at Gunpowder. We think it'll become a favorite in your home, too. *Photographed overleaf.*

1 head of broccoli, halved
½ cup Greek yogurt
¼ cup full-fat cream cheese
2 tablespoons whole grain mustard
½ teaspoon chile powder
1 teaspoon chaat masala
1 teaspoon turmeric powder
½ teaspoon ground coriander
¼ teaspoon ground cumin
2 tablespoons mustard or canola oil, plus 1 teaspoon
1 tablespoon chickpea flour
2–3 tablespoons ghee, melted
sea salt
Makhani Sauce (see right) and pickled beet, to serve

1 Bring a pot of salted water to a boil and cook the broccoli for 3 minutes, then drain and rinse under ice-cold water to prevent it from cooking further. Shake off any excess water and let sit.

2 In a large dish, mix the yogurt, cream cheese, mustard, chile powder, chaat masala, turmeric, cilantro, cumin, and 3 tablespoons of mustard or canola oil.

3 Set a skillet over medium heat and toast the chickpea flour for 30 seconds. Add the remaining 1 teaspoon of oil, mix, and toast for an additional 30 seconds, making a fragrant paste. Whisk this into the yogurt mix, then thoroughly coat the broccoli in the creamy spice paste and let sit to marinade for 30 minutes.

4 Set your oven broiler to high and broil the broccoli, cut-side down, for 10–15 minutes, basting it with melted ghee. When golden on top, turn over and broil for an additional 5 minutes on the other side, or until nicely colored.

5 Serve on a base of Makhani Sauce (see right) with pickled beetroot sprinkled on top.

Although here we are serving it with our famous Mustard Broccoli, this sauce is also a lovely accompaniment to our Kale and Corn Cakes (see page 18) or any grilled meat, especially lamb.

2 tablespoons unsalted butter
2 garlic cloves, finely minced
2 teaspoons freshly grated ginger
2½ cups (1 pound) tomatoes, diced
½ teaspoon ground fenugreek seeds
½ teaspoon cumin seeds
3 cloves
3 cardamom pods
¼ teaspoon freshly ground black pepper
a pinch of chile powder
¼ teaspoon freshly grated nutmeg
2–3 tablespoons heavy cream
1 teaspoon honey (optional)
sea salt

1 Set a skillet over high heat and add 1 tablespoon of the butter. Once melted, add the garlic, ginger, and a pinch of salt and cook for a minute.

2 Fold the tomatoes and all the spices through. Cook over medium heat until the tomatoes have broken down and darkened in a color a little, about 5–10 minutes.

3 Spoon the mixture into a food processor or blender and purée until fairly smooth. Press through a strainer, giving you a smooth sauce. Warm the sauce gently in a pot with the remaining tablespoon of butter. Once the butter is melted, swirl in the cream.

4 Let the sauce gently bubble away over medium-low heat for about 5 minutes until it has thickened and darkened further. Season with salt and the honey, if needed, to taste. Serve warm.

# EGGPLANT BHARTA

Nobody, and I mean nobody, makes this dish like my mother and my grandmother. We joke that you must have the last name Baweja to make this dish well, but here we've given away our family secret. Two extra tips to make this dish a hit. First, mash the eggplant with a fork rather than chopping it with a knife. Second, use the core of the eggplant—this part has the most flavor but for some reason people tend to throw it away—and don't be afraid to keep a few bits of the burnt skin, too.

1 large (1¾ pound) or 2 small (14 ounce) eggplants
½ teaspoon canola or olive oil
1 tablespoon ghee
1 teaspoon cumin seeds
2 medium-sized onions, thinly sliced
1½ teaspoons freshly grated ginger
1 garlic clove, finely chopped
½ green chile, finely chopped
1 large or 2 medium tomatoes, finely diced
½ teaspoon turmeric
1 tablespoon ground cumin
1 tablespoon ground coriander
½ tablespoon garam masala (store-bought, or see page 161)
3 tablespoons fresh cilantro, finely chopped
sea salt

1 Rub the eggplant(s) with oil and roast for about 15 minutes over an open flame until charred all over and tender all the way through, turning often. You can finish it off in an oven preheated to 400°F if it's nicely charred but not tender enough. Let sit to cool.

2 Strip the eggplant of its charred skin— it should come off easily with your hands or when scraped with a spoon. Discard the skin and mash the pulp thoroughly, then let sit.

3 Place the ghee in a pan over medium heat and add the cumin seeds. When they crackle, add the onions and gently cook for about 1 minute until golden brown. Add the ginger, garlic, and green chile, and sauté for a few more seconds. Stir in the tomato, turmeric, cumin and ground coriander and cook for an additionalminute, then fold in the mashed eggplant and garam masala and cook for 3–4 minutes.

4 Season with sea salt, to taste, and serve warm with the chopped fresh cilantro scattered on top.

GUNPOWDER

PLEASE WAIT
TO BE
SEATED

THANK YOU

# GUNPOWDER ALOO CHAAT

SERVES 4

This dish reminds me of my winter holidays. We'd go to Delhi and this would be the first dish we'd eat in the markets. Every region of India has their own version. In this one, the potatoes are fried, which gives them a wonderful crust. The vendors in the markets make them with so much drama, flattening the hot, boiled potatoes before smashing them into the pan of sizzling ghee. Ah, the aroma when they are cooking is amazing. In the east, aloo chaat is made with boiled potatoes but it really can't compete with this.

FOR THE GUNPOWDER ALOO
20 baby new potatoes, washed
½ cup sunflower or canola oil, for frying
1–2 tablespoons Gunpowder Spice Mix
    (see page 158)

FOR THE SWEET YOGURT
¾ cup Greek yogurt
1 teaspoon superfine sugar

FOR THE SPICED TAMARIND AND DATE CHUTNEY
2 ounces tamarind paste
½ cup pitted dates
¼ cup jaggery or raw sugar
¼ teaspoon ground cumin
¼ teaspoon ground coriander
½ teaspoon freshly grated ginger
a pinch of chile powder
sea salt

FOR THE BLACK HORSE GRAM SALAD
2½ cups cooked black horse gram
    beans (see page 10) or
    French green lentils
2 tomatoes, finely chopped
1 red onion, finely chopped
1 green chile, or more or less, to taste
½ teaspoon black salt
1 teaspoon mango powder

TO GARNISH
4 thin rounds of peeled fresh lotus root
micro cilantro leaves

1 Wash and boil the baby potatoes in salted water for 25 minutes or until tender all the way through. Drain, cool, and then gently press each potato flat so that it looks like a little potato cake. Let sit.

2 In a bowl, mix together the yogurt and sugar and let sit.

3 Place the tamarind, dates, and 1 cup of water in a blender and purée until smooth. Transfer this mixture to a pot and simmer until warmed through, then add the jaggery or brown sugar and spices, season with salt, and cook over medium heat for 5–10 minutes until it darkens and thickens to the consistency of ketchup. Strain through a strainer and let sit.

4 In a large bowl, toss all the salad ingredients together.

5 In a large skillet, heat the oil over high heat and fry the potato cakes for about 3–4 minutes until golden and crisp on both sides. Fry the lotus root rounds in the same oil for 1 minute until golden and crisp, then remove and drain on paper towels.

6 Divide the fried potatoes between serving plates and top each plate with 3 tablespoons of the black horse gram salad, followed by a sprinkling of gunpowder spice. Top with a drizzle of the sweet yogurt and tamarind chutney, followed by a small spoon of salad. Garnish with a lotus root crisp and a scattering of micro cilantro leaves.

# CHENNA PATURI

SERVES 4

Chenna paturi is a traditional dish of paneer that's rubbed with a punchy paste made with mustard, coconut, and green chiles. This is a vegetarian adaption of the popular Bengali fish recipe paturi, one of the royal dishes of Bengali cuisine. Sometimes large pumpkin leaves are used in place of banana leaves. You can make this with either.

20 ounces paneer, cut into 4 even pieces
1 cup wholegrain mustard
2 tablespoons mustard oil or rapeseed oil
5 tablespoons freshly squeezed lemon juice
5 tablespoons freshly grated or
    dessicated coconut
2 tablespoons grated fresh ginger
4 garlic cloves, finely minced
1 green chile, finely chopped
1 teaspoon Kashmiri chile powder (see Tip)
2 tablespoons turmeric powder
1 vegetable stock cube
4 (9-inch) square pieces of banana leaf

1  Take a bowl and mix the mustard, oil, lemon juice, coconut, ginger, garlic, green chile, chile powder, turmeric, and stock cube to a make a coarse paste.

2  Add the paneer pieces and mix until evenly coated. Cover and keep them in the refrigerator for 2–3 hours to marinade.

3  Gently warm the banana leaves over an open flame for 10–20 seconds on both sides, ensuring they don't get burnt.

4  Place a piece of marinated paneer in the middle of each banana leaf square and fold the leaf around it, making an envelope (you can tie the envelope with string).

5  Set the paneer parcels in a steamer basket and steam for 25 minutes. Alternatively, you can place them in a warm, lidded skillet with 2 tablespoons water and steam.

6  Once the paneer is steamed, remove from the heat and let sit. Set a large, dry skillet or griddle pan over high heat. Grill each paneer parcel for 2 minutes on each side until it is marked by the grill. Serve hot.

TIP

Kashmiri chile powder can be made by grinding whole dried Kashmiri chiles to a powder. Alternatively, use half the amount (or less) or normal chile powder as Kashmiri chiles are quite mild and fruity in comparison.

# BULGUR MOONG SALAD

SERVES 2–4

This recipe is from Nirmal's family. It's made with lighter, cheaper ingredients from his village and is a good way to balance lots of heavy dishes.

FOR THE SALAD
½ cup bulgur wheat, soaked overnight
   in enough fresh water to fully cover
½ cup yellow moong dal, soaked overnight
   in enough fresh water to fully cover
1 tablespoon freshly grated ginger
2 scallions, finely chopped
1 tomato, deseeded and finely diced
juice of 1 lime
sea salt, to taste

FOR THE DRESSING
4 tablespoons olive or canola oil
2 garlic cloves, finely minced
8 mint leaves, finely chopped

1  First make the dressing. Heat the oil in a skillet until just smoking, then take it off the heat. Let sit to cool a little, then add the garlic. When the oil is completely cooled, add the chopped mint and let sit to infuse for 2 hours. Strain into a jug and reserve until ready to use.

2  Drain the bulgur wheat and moong dal and rinse with fresh water, then transfer to a large bowl.

3  In a large bowl, mix together all the salad ingredients and season with salt, to taste. Toss with the dressing and serve.

# CHUTNEY CHEESE SANDWICH

SERVES 4

My family are members of a huge golf club in India. In fact, it's the largest golf club outside the UK. When we go, we play golf all day and the loser has to buy the others breakfast. We used to get these bland toasted cheese sandwiches at the club and I would always complain, so the chef added this wonderful fresh chutney, and BOOM—it was a whole new dish! I could eat this everyday.

5–6 tablespoons butter
¼ green pepper, finely chopped
¼ red pepper, finely chopped
¼ red onion, finely chopped
3½ ounces mild cheddar cheese, grated
7 ounces mozzarella cheese, torn
a pinch of chile powder
8 thick slices of bread

FOR THE MINT AND CILANTRO CHUTNEY
½ cup fresh mint, finely chopped
½ ounce cilantro, finely chopped
½ cup grated fresh coconut (see Note
  on page 51)
1 green chile, finely chopped
2 teaspoons cumin seeds, toasted
3 tablespoons freshly squeezed lime juice
a pinch of dry ginger powder or
  ¼ teaspoon freshly grated ginger
sea salt, to taste

1 In a bowl, mix together all the ingredients for the mint and cilantro chutney and then let sit.

2 Heat 1 tablespoon of the butter in a non-stick sauté pan, add the peppers and onion, and sauté for 5 minutes or until tender. Remove from the heat and transfer to a bowl. Add the cheese, chile powder and half of the green chutney. Mix well.

3 Use the remaining butter to lightly butter one side of each of the bread slices and pile the cheese mix on four of the slices. Cover with the remaining bread to make four sandwiches.

4 Heat a sandwich toaster or set a large skillet over high heat. Add a generous slick of butter to the sandwich toaster or the skillet and toast the sandwiches until golden on each side, adding more butter, if necessary.

5 Serve hot with the remaining mint and cilantro chutney on the side.

# KADAI PANEER POCKET

SERVES 4–6

In every Indian bakery you can see items that are clearly inspired by French pâtissiers, but of course, there's always an Indian twist. This is a classic example. You've got all that wonderful, buttery, flaky pastry, yet housed inside is Indian cheese and fragrant spices.

14 ounces ready-rolled puff pastry, fully defrosted if frozen
1 teaspoon canola or olive oil
1 onion, finely chopped
1 teaspoon freshly grated ginger
1 garlic clove, finely minced
1 red pepper, finely diced
1 green pepper, finely diced
14 ounces paneer, diced
¼ teaspoon ground cumin
½ teaspoon ground coriander
½ teaspoon turmeric powder
½ teaspoon chaat masala
¼ teaspoon mango powder
a pinch of chile powder or chile flakes
4 tablespoons freshly chopped cilantro
sea salt

1  Preheat the oven to 400°F. Line a baking sheet with parchment paper.

2  Set a skillet over medium heat. Add the oil and swirl in the onion. Cook for 10 minutes or until tender and a little golden.

3  Stir in the ginger and garlic, then add the peppers and a little salt. Mix well, cover, and cook for 2–3 minutes until the peppers are tender.

4  Take off the heat. Fold in the paneer, all the spices, and the chopped cilantro. Mix well.

5  Unroll the pastry sheets. Put all the stuffing in the center and fold the pastry over the filling lengthways, so that you have a long, thin rectangular shape.

6  Use a fork to gently, but firmly, press into the edges to help seal. Cut equally into 2-inch portions.

7  Arrange the parcels on the prepared baking sheet. Bake for 15 minutes or until golden and puffed up. Transfer to a cooling rack to rest for 5 minutes before serving. These are delicious served with the Makhani Sauce (see page 31) and crispy kale—this is how we serve it in the restaurant.

TIPS
Use any vegetable and spice combination for the pockets. It is very important to leave them to cool for 5 minutes—this will make the puffs nice and flaky AND they won't burn your mouth. If you don't have a cooling rack, improvise—prop an oven rack above the work surface and use that.

# PUNJABI CHANA MASALA

I'm Punjabi and every good Punjabi boy loves chana masala. It's an easy vegetable dish, and pure comfort food. Serve with rice, raita or chutney, and a salad.

5 tablespoons canola or olive oil
1 tablespoon freshly grated ginger
1–2 green chiles, finely chopped
ground seeds from 3 black cardamom pods
½ cinnamon stick
2 onions, finely chopped
4 garlic cloves, finely minced
2 tomatoes, finely chopped
2 teaspoons ground coriander
1½ teaspoons garam masala (store-bought, or see page 161)
½ teaspoon chile powder, to taste
4 teaspoons Chana Masala (see page 10)
4 cups (21 ounces) cooked chickpeas, drained and rinsed
1 teaspoon fenugreek leaves
5 tablespoons freshly chopped cilantro
sea salt
bread, to serve

1 Heat the oil in a deep non-stick skillet over medium heat, add the ginger, green chiles, ground cardamom, and cinnamon stick, and cook, stirring, for 30 seconds.

2 Add the onions and garlic and sauté for 5 minutes until the onions are soft and a little golden. Add the chopped tomatoes, mix well, and cook for 3 minutes, stirring occasionally. Fold the ground coriander, garam masala, chile powder and chana masala into the vegetables and cook for an additional minute, stirring occasionally.

3 Add the chickpeas, fenugreek, 1¾ cup of water, and a pinch of salt. Stir everything together and cook over medium heat for 15–20 minutes, stirring occasionally, or until the water dries out.

4 Serve warm, scattered with the chopped fresh cilantro and your choice of bread.

# TANDOORI PANEER AND SAAG

SERVES 2–4

These are two staple dishes in my family. In my house, we would either ha```ve the spinach sauce, which we call *saag*, or the tandoori paneer, but they were never served together. They do, however, make the perfect marriage, so I'm happy to unite them here.

FOR THE TANDOORI PANEER
2 teaspoons chickpea flour
1 teaspoon mustard or canola oil
½ teaspoon freshly squeezed
   lemon juice
⅔ cup Greek or natural yogurt
1 teaspoon freshly grated ginger
2 garlic cloves, finely minced
1 green chile, finely chopped
a pinch of chile powder
½ teaspoon black cumin seeds
½ teaspoon carom seeds
1 teaspoon turmeric powder
2 teaspoons chaat masala
1 teaspoon kasoori methi
3 tablespoons finely chopped
   cilantro
17 ounces paneer, cut into 1-inch
   cubes
chile flakes, to serve
sea salt

FOR THE SAAG
2 pounds baby leaf spinach, washed
   and drained
4 tablespoons canola or olive oil
2 teaspoons cumin seeds
2 dried red chiles
2 onions, finely chopped
6 garlic cloves, finely chopped
1 thumb-sized piece of ginger,
   peeled and julienned
1 green chile, finely chopped
½ teaspoon turmeric powder
3 tablespoons freshly grated tomato
2 teaspoons Malvani Garam Masala
   (see page 161)
1 teaspoon mango powder (optional
4 tablespoons light cream
3 tablespoons butter

1 For the tandoori paneer, place a skillet over medium heat. Add the chickpea flour and toast for 30 seconds, then take off the heat and fold in the oil and lemon juice to make a paste. Stir in the yogurt and all the remaining ingredients, apart from the paneer, salt and chile flakes. Mix everything together, then add the paneer and coat thoroughly in the mix. Dust with a sprinkling of salt and let sit to marinate for 1 hour.

2 For the saag, blanch the spinach in a pot of boiling water, then drain, refresh with cold water and let sit to cool. Transfer to a blender and purée until smooth, then let sit.

3 Preheat your oven broiler to high.

4 Meanwhile, heat the oil in a skillet over medium heat. Add the cumin seeds and dried chile and stir through the oil for 30 seconds, then add the onions and cook for 5–10 minutes or until soft and glossy.

5 Add the garlic, ginger, green chile, and turmeric, and sauté for a minute, then fold in the tomato pulp and cook down for 1–2 minutes until the tomato has thickened to a paste.

6 Add the garam masala, mango powder (if using), cream, and butter and, as soon as the butter is melted, fold through the spinach, then take off the heat and let sit.

7 Arrange the marinated paneer on a grill pan and flash under the hot broiler, cooking for 3 minutes on each side or until lightly charred all over. Alternatively, you can heat a little oil in a non-stick skillet and fry the paneer over medium heat.

8 Gently warm the saag through before serving, then spoon a little into the bottom of each serving bowl and top with the grilled paneer. A sprinkling of chile flakes finishes this dish off to perfection.

# CILANTRO-SPICED
# ROAST VEG SALAD
## with WALNUTS

SERVES 4

My mother is a vegetarian and like any good mother she was always trying to get more vegetables into our diet. She used to roast up great big trays of vegetables sprinkled with fragrant spices. This was her way of enticing us, and it worked. Nirmal has dressed this up a bit further with the walnuts and the dressing. It's a great dish for the whole family.

½ butternut squash, peeled, deseeded, and
    cut into 1-inch pieces
1 zucchini, chopped into 1-inch pieces
1 red pepper, chopped into 1-inch pieces
1 bulb of fennel, chopped into 1-inch pieces
3 tablespoons canola or olive oil
3 tablespoons freshly squeezed lime juice
2 teaspoons freshly ground black pepper
3½ ounces walnuts
3½ ounces mixed salad leaves
sea salt

FOR THE DRESSING
½ ounce freshly chopped cilantro
1 teaspoon freshly grated ginger
2 garlic cloves, finely minced
½ teaspoon superfine sugar
½ green chile
1 tablespoon raw mango (or rehydrate
    a slice of dried mango)
5 tablespoons canola or olive oil
sea salt

1 Preheat your oven to 400°F and place a roasting pan on the middle shelf to heat up.

2 In a bowl, toss the chopped vegetables with the oil, lime juice, black pepper, and a good pinch of sea salt, then pour into the preheated roasting tin and roast for 25–30 minutes, or until the vegetables are tender and a little charred around the edges.

3 For the dressing, whisk together all the ingredients in a bowl, adding the oil gradually as you blend. If the consistency is a little thick, thin out with a little water. Season with salt, to taste.

4 Spread the walnuts out on a baking sheet and roast in the still-hot oven for about 5 minutes, until fragrant.

5 In a large bowl, toss together the roasted vegetables with the dressing and salad leaves. Divide between serving plates and scatter with the roasted walnuts.

# CABBAGE AND COCONUT SALAD

SERVES 4

Nirmal's mother gave us this recipe. He grew up in the Chini Chini village on the Gujarati border, where this dish is popular, especially in family homes. It's a really simple dish and a beautiful way to eat cabbage. It's lovely on its own, or paired with rice or fish.

3 tablespoons coconut oil
1½ teaspoons yellow mustard seeds
1½ teaspoons white urad dal, well rinsed
10 curry leaves (fresh are best if you can get them, but dried are fine)
4 green chiles, sliced on the diagonal
2 teaspoons freshly grated ginger
½ large or 1 small cabbage, finely shredded
1 teaspoon sugar
½ teaspoon turmeric powder
freshly grated flesh from 1 coconut (see Note)
1 teaspoon freshly squeezed lemon juice
a good pinch of sea salt

1 Heat the oil in a non-stick skillet, add the mustard seeds and wait for them to pop. Add the urad dal, curry leaves, green chiles, and ginger, and sauté over medium heat for a few seconds, stirring continuously.

2 Add the shredded cabbage, sugar, turmeric, and salt. Mix well and cook for 8–10 minutes, stirring once or twice. Add the coconut, reduce the heat and cook gently, stirring continuously, for 1–2 minutes. Sprinkle over the lemon juice and serve warm.

NOTE
To remove the flesh from a coconut, wrap the coconut in a clean dish towel. Set it in a metal bowl, still wrapped in the towel, and bash it a few times with a hammer or rolling pin until it cracks. Lift the coconut, and the dish towel should strain out all the juice. Drink it or save for another use. Use the tip of a butter knife to prise the flesh from the coconut skin. Grate the flesh using a box grater or the grating attachment on your food processor.

# BHUNA EGGPLANT
# AND CRISPY KALE SALAD

SERVES 2 AS A LIGHT MAIN, 4 AS A STARTER

Nirmal has a magical way with vegetables. Keen to introduce some lighter dishes onto the menu, he's created some amazing salads taking inspiration from English ingredients but adding Indian flavors. It's not often you see mango mixed with kale. Trust me, it works.

4 cups sunflower oil for frying
5 ounces kale, destalked, washed and finely chopped
1 eggplant, chopped into 1-inch pieces
1 tablespoon mango powder
1 tablespoon black salt (or 1 teaspoon sea salt)
½ teaspoon cumin seeds, toasted
⅓ cup Greek yogurt
1½-inch chunk of cucumber
8 ounces cherry tomatoes, halved
3½ ounces pomegranate seeds
1 mango, sliced
sea salt, to taste

1 Heat the oil in a deep, heavy-bottomed pot over high heat. You want the temperature to reach 350°F. If you don't have a thermometer, you can test that the oil is hot enough by dropping a grain of rice in the oil; if the rice floats to the top and has bubbles around it, your oil is ready for frying.

2 Fry the kale in the hot oil, in small batches, until it's crispy. Remove with a slotted spoon and drain on paper towels. Sprinkle each batch with a pinch of salt.

3 Keep the oil hot and fry the eggplant cubes, in small batches, until golden on all sides. Remove with a slotted spoon, drain on paper towels, and sprinkle with half the mango powder and black or sea salt.

4 In a bowl, whisk the yogurt with the remaining mango powder, black salt, and half the toasted cumin seeds. Coarsely grate the cucumber, place in a strainer, and squeeze out as much water as you can. Mix into the yogurt—and you have a cucumber raita.

5 To assemble the salad, spread a little cucumber raita over the base of your serving plates. Layer the cherry tomatoes on top, followed by the fried eggplant pieces and crispy kale. Finish with the pomegranate seeds, the mango and the remaining toasted cumin seeds. Serve straight away.

# BANANA FLOWER AND
# SABUDANA CROQUETTES

SERVES 4

Nirmal loves banana flowers—they're one of his favorite ingredients. You can see the fresh flower in all its glory on page two of this book. It not only looks beautiful but it tastes wonderful, too. If you can't get hold of fresh banana flower, you can find it canned (see Note), which works just as well. This is the first dish Nirmal ever made for me. I love it.

1 medium fresh banana flower (see note)
1 teaspoon turmeric powder
1 large potato, boiled until fully tender
1 tablespoon freshly grated ginger
½ teaspoon ground cumin
3 tablespoons canola or sunflower oil, plus extra for deep frying
a pinch of finely chopped green chile
3 tablespoons raisins, soaked in enough boiling water to cover for 15 minutes
4 tablespoons toasted coconut flakes
½ teaspoon superfine sugar
2 teaspoons garam masala (store-bought, or see page 161)
4 tablespoons roasted peanuts, lightly crushed
5 ounces tapioca pearls, soaked overnight
5 tablespoons cornstarch
2 cups Panko breadcrumbs
sea salt

1  Prepare your banana blossom. To do this, chop the blossom and place in a bowl of water with ½ teaspoon turmeric powder—otherwise the blossoms will turn black. Wash the blossom in this water. Bring a pot of salted water to the boil. Add the remaining ½ teaspoon turmeric powder to the water, along with the washed blossom.

2  Cook, covered, for 8–10 minutes or until the flower is soft but not mushy. Please monitor this, as some flowers might take less time, and some more. Drain in a colander and lightly mash the blossom with the back of your spatula.

3  Peel and mash the boiled potato with salt, to taste, until smooth. Let sit.

4  Mix the ginger and cumin with 2 teaspoons water to make a paste.

5  Set a skillet over medium heat. Add the 3 tablespoons oil. Once hot, stir in the chile, followed by the ginger and cumin paste. Mix in the mashed banana blossom with a  pinch of salt and cook for 6–8 minutes.

6  Drain the soaked raisins and add them to the pan, along with the mashed potato, toasted coconut, and sugar. Cook for a minute and take off heat.

7  Mix the garam masala, peanuts, and drained tapioca into the banana mix. Once the mixture is cool enough to handle, roll small portions between your palms into golf ball-sized croquette shapes. Transfer to the refrigerator for 15 minutes.

8  Whisk the cornstarch with 5 tablespoons water to make a smooth, milk-like batter. Place the breadcrumbs on a flat plate.

9  Dip the croquettes in the cornstarch mix and immediately roll in breadcrumbs, ensuring that all sides are thoroughly covered with the crumbs. Place on a clean plate.

10  At this stage, you can store the croquettes in the refrigerator for 3–4 days in an airtight container. Try to arrange them in a single layer to maintain the shapes.

11  Once you are ready to cook, heat enough oil for deep-frying in a deep, heavy-bottomed pan over medium heat. Deep-fry the croquettes (in batches if necessary) for 5 minutes until the outer layer is deep golden and crisp.

12  These are delicious served with raita and salad.

### NOTE

You can use canned banana blossom if you can't find fresh—it is available online or in specialist Indian stores. You need 10 ounces (drained weight).

SMALL PLATES

55

# SOUTH INDIAN CURD RICE

SERVES 4

Any time you have an upset stomach back home, this is what is served. The rice and yogurt have a soothing effect and the spices used are healing. Of course, you don't need to wait until you're suffering from an upset stomach to enjoy this! Eat it anytime—it's especially good with pickles on the side, or served as a cooling companion to a spicy dish.

1½ cups cooked brown or white basmati rice
¾ cup natural or Greek yogurt
3 tablespoons coconut or canola oil
3 teaspoons yellow mustard seed
1 teaspoon white urad dal, rinsed well
1 green chile, finely chopped
6 curry leaves (fresh are best if you can get them, but dried are fine)
2 tablespoons freshly chopped cilantro
sea salt

1 In a bowl, stir 1 tablespoon water into the rice and mash lightly using a potato masher. Mix in the yogurt and a pinch of salt, then cover and refrigerate for 1 hour.

2 Heat the oil in a small non-stick skillet, add the mustard seeds and urad dal, and sauté over medium heat for 30 seconds. Add the green chile and curry leaves and sauté for 30 seconds.

3 Fold the cilantro through the chilled rice, then spoon over the oil and tempered spices. Serve straight away alongside a spicy meat dish, such as the Goan Pork on page 93.

# ROASTED BHUTTA

SERVES 2

On the streets of India, people from the villages come to the market with portable barbecues when the sweet corn comes into season because it's so fresh that you want to cook it then and there. The smell of the sweet butter fills the air and travels for miles, and the crack of the corn meeting the dancing flames is so hypnotic.

2 whole corn cobs
1½ tablespoons salted butter
a pinch of freshly ground black pepper

COCONUT CHILE AND CILANTRO DRIZZLE
5 tablespoons grated fresh coconut
3 tablespoons freshly chopped cilantro
a good pinch of chile powder
a pinch of garlic salt
1½ tablespoons freshly squeezed lime juice
½ teaspoon canola or olive oil

1  Remove the husk and silk from the corn, but keep the stem intact, which will help you handle the corn when you roast it.

2  Prepare a charcoal barbecue. Spread the butter over the corn and sprinkle with black pepper. Grill the corn over the barbecue for 10–15 minutes, rotating often to cook each side evenly. Alternatively, preheat the oven to 400°F. Wrap the corn in foil and roast for 20–25 minutes.

3  While the corn cooks, mix the coconut with the cilantro in a small bowl. In a separate bowl, whisk together the chile powder, garlic salt, lime juice, and oil.

4  Serve the roasted corn hot with the dressing drizzled all over the top. Finish with a generous sprinkle of the fresh coconut and cilantro.

# MASALA BHAAT

SERVES 6

Nirmal's wife wooed him with this dish. In India, cooking for someone is the ultimate expression of love. This one clearly won Nirmal over. It's a dish he loves serving and sharing with the customers at Gunpowder.

1 teaspoon coriander seeds
6 cloves
10 black peppercorns
2 teaspoons cumin seeds
3 tablespoons canola or olive oil
2 onions, finely chopped
5 tablespoons freshly grated ginger
3 green chiles, finely chopped (more or less, to taste)
½ teaspoon turmeric powder
a pinch of asafoetida
1 eggplant, cut into ½-inch dice
1½ cups basmati rice, soaked for 15 minutes
4 ounces green beans, trimmed and cut into 1½-inch pieces
¾ cup (4 ounces) green peas
6 tablespoons freshly chopped cilantro
raita (see pages 176–183) or yogurt, to serve
sea salt

1 Heat a non-stick skillet over medium heat and toast the coriander seeds, cloves, black peppercorns, and half the cumin seeds for a few seconds. Remove from the heat and allow to cool a little, transfer to a spice or coffee grinder or a mortar and pestle and grind to a powder. Let sit.

2 Heat the oil in a deep pot, add the remaining cumin seeds, and sauté the onions for 5–10 minutes until soft and golden. Fold in the ginger and chile and cook for a minute, then add the turmeric, asafoetida, eggplant, and a good pinch of salt and fry for 10 minutes or until tender.

3 Stir in the rice, beans, and peas. Add 2½ cups hot water and the ground spice mix you prepared earlier and mix well, then cover with a tightly fitting lid. Cook for 12–15 minutes or until all the water is absorbed by the rice.

4 Take off the heat and leave to steam for an additional 5–10 minutes, then stir the chopped cilantro through and serve with raita or just natural yogurt.

NOTE

In India, this would commonly be cooked with cluster beans. They look like smaller, flatter French green beans. If you can find them, they are great for this dish, but regular green beans work just as well.

# BEEF PEPPER FRY

For work, my dad had to go to South India a lot and this was a dish he came across in one of the canteens he'd stop by for food. For ten rupees you get the basic rice, lentils, and salad. You then get to choose a meat or a fish to go alongside. I would sometimes travel with my dad on these trips and this was always one of my favorite canteen dishes.

2 rump or blade steaks (approx. 9 ounces each), thinly sliced
3 tablespoons freshly grated ginger
1 green chile, finely chopped
4 garlic cloves, finely chopped
2 teaspoons freshly ground black pepper
½ teaspoon ground coriander
½ teaspoon turmeric powder
a pinch of chile powder
2 whole dried red chiles
4 tablespoons coconut oil
1 teaspoon yellow mustard seed
15 fresh curry leaves (dried will also work)
2 onions, thinly sliced
1 ounce freshly chopped cilantro
½ cup coconut flakes, toasted
1 lime, cut into wedges

1 Place the sliced beef in a bowl with the ginger, green chile, garlic, black pepper, ground coriander, turmeric, and chile powder and, using your fingers, massage the spices into the meat.

2 Set a skillet with a lid over high heat. When hot, add the beef and dried chiles (no oil is needed), cover and cook for 5–10 minutes or until the beef is cooked through. Remove the lid and continue cooking until all the moisture cooks down and coats the meat.

3 Meanwhile, in a separate pan, heat the coconut oil and add the mustard seeds and curry leaves. Let them sizzle for a few seconds, then add the onions and fry for about 5 minutes until golden brown. Fold in the cooked beef and chopped cilantro and cook, stirring occasionally, for an additional 5–10 minutes, until the beef pepper fry turns a dark brown color.

4 Serve immediately with the toasted coconut flakes and lime wedges on the side.

# GRILLED EGGPLANT
## with LAMB KEEMA and PINE NUT KACHUMBER

SERVES 4

Nirmal took part in a Cook for Syria fundraising event and this is the dish he created. It's a delicious and fragrant marriage of Indian and Persian spices.

FOR THE LAMB KEEMA
2 cinnamon sticks
3 cardamom pods, bruised
5 cloves
3 tablespoons canola or olive oil
2 onions, finely chopped
1 tablespoon freshly grated ginger
3 garlic cloves, finely chopped
1 green chile chopped
3 tablespoons ground coriander
½ teaspoon garam masala (store-bought, or see page 161)
½ teaspoon turmeric powder
½ teaspoon chile powder
1 teaspoon ground cumin
2 large tomatoes, finely chopped
1 pound ground lamb
5 tablespoons freshly chopped cilantro

FOR THE PINE NUT KACHUMBER
¾ cup pine nuts
2 teaspoons canola or olive oil
⅔ cup scallions, finely chopped
1 green chile, finely chopped
1 tomato, finely diced
2 tablespoons freshly chopped cilantro
sea salt, to taste

FOR THE EGGPLANT
2 large eggplants
1 tablespoon canola or olive oil
2 teaspoons freshly ground black peppe

1 Set a large skillet over medium heat. Add the cinnamon, cardamom, and cloves and dry-fry for 30 seconds. Add the oil and onion and sauté for 5 minutes, stirring occasionally, until golden brown.

2 Stir in the ginger, garlic, and chile. Cook for a minute, then add all the ground spices. Cook for an additionalminute.

3 Add the chopped tomatoes, stir, and leave to simmer for 10–15 minutes or until the tomatoes have cooked down into a fairly thick paste.

4 Add the ground lamb and cook over high heat for 5 minutes, stirring continuously. Reduce the heat to a gentle simmer and cook, covered, for about 10 minutes. Uncover and cook over high heat for an additional 5–10 minutes or until the mixture is fairly dry. Fold in the freshly chopped cilantro. Let sit.

5 In a bowl, mix together all the ingredients for the pine nut kachumber. Season with salt, to taste.

6 Preheat your oven broiler to high. Thinly slice the eggplant lengthways. Brush lightly with the oil and arrange on a grill pan. Cook under the grill for 4 minutes on each side, or until nicely golden. Season with the black pepper and a good pinch of salt.

7 Serve the beef mince on the top of the grilled eggplant, with the the pine nut kachumber sprinkled over the top.

# NAGALAND HOUSE BABY PORK RIBS

SERVES 4

My younger brother Avneet has a friend from Nagaland and his mother used to make this pork dish. We were lucky to get her recipe. You will love this dish. Of course, if you can't find naga or ghost chiles, you can use any other chile, and add more or less to suit to your taste. The different layers of cooking in this recipe are what make it so special.

3 cups apple juice
5 ounces freshly grated ginger
2–3 naga chiles, split down the center
8 whole star anise
a slice of fresh orange
⅓ cup brown sugar
2 pounds baby back pork ribs
4 cups sunflower oil, for frying

FOR THE NAGA BBQ SAUCE
Half the leftover stock from the braised ribs
⅓ cup ketchup
½ cup cider vinegar
3 tablespoons honey
½ cup light brown sugar
1 tablespoon tamarind concentrate
1 teaspoon crushed dried naga chiles,
   to taste
sea salt and freshly ground black pepper

FOR THE KACHUMBER SALAD
1 red onion
4 scallions
1 tomato
½ cucumber, finely diced

TO SERVE
1 lime
a handful of fresh cilantro, chopped

1 In a large pot with a lid, combine the apple juice, grated ginger, chiles, star anise, orange, and brown sugar, stirring to mix well. Add the pork ribs and cover with about 6 cups water. Place over high heat and bring to the boil, then simmer over low heat for about 2½ hours, turning the ribs a few times, until tender.

2 Lift the ribs out of the stock, place on a chopping board, and leave to cool. With a sharp knife, cut in-between the ribs at two-rib intervals.

3 Strain half of the stock into a fresh pot (discard the remaining stock or reserve it for use in another recipe). Add the ketchup, cider vinegar, honey, sugar, tamarind, and chiles and bring to the boil, then simmer over low heat, stirring occasionally, until thickened, about 45 minutes. Season with salt and black pepper, to taste, then strain the sauce through a fine strainer into a bowl.

4 In a separate bowl, toss together all the ingredients for the kachumber salad.

5 Heat the oil in a deep, heavy-bottomed pot over high heat. Deep-fry the ribs in batches for 5 minutes until crispy and then dip into the sauce to glaze. Serve garnished with the kachumber salad, with a squeeze of lime and the chopped cilantro, along with the remaining sauce for dipping.

TIPS

The cooked ribs can be refrigerated in their braising liquid overnight and reheated gently before grilling. The sauce can be stored in the refrigerator for up to 1 week.

# TAWA KALIMIRCH CHICKEN

SERVES 2–4

The marinade for the chicken here is very traditional. We would always have this at home—often with a whole chicken or with two wings and two breasts. The avocado dip gives it a modern twist—a very delicious one. It's a complete hit in the restaurant and is a quick dish to make at home.

2 boneless, skinless chicken breasts, sliced
1 tablespoon canola or olive oil

FOR THE MARINADE
3 tablespoons canola or olive oil
2 green chiles, to taste
1 teaspoon tamarind paste
1 tablespoon freshly grated dinger
2 garlic cloves, finely minced
½ teaspoon freshly ground black pepper
½ cinnamon stick
2 cloves
sea salt, to taste

FOR THE AVOCADO DIP
1 ripe avocado
3½ ounces freshly chopped cilantro
3 tablespoons fresh mango
1 teaspoon freshly grated ginger
1 garlic clove, finely minced
½ teaspoon superfine sugar
1 green chile, finely chopped
sea salt, to taste

1 Place all the marinade ingredients in a blender and blend until smooth. Tip the marinade over the chicken slices and massage into the meat with your hands. Cover and place in the refrigerator for 2 hours or overnight.

2 Put all the dip ingredients in a blender and blend until smooth, adding 1 tablespoon water if necessary.

3 Heat the oil in a large skillet and cook the chicken for 3–4 minutes on each side until cooked through. Serve warm with the avocado dip.

# GINGER CHICKEN WINGS

SERVES 4

This is Nirmal's favorite recipe, he's crazy about chicken wings! Given the chance, he'd eat them every day for breakfast, lunch, and dinner. This is, of course, a gourmet version—and the best you'll taste.

2 pounds chicken wings
2 large thumb-sized pieces of
　ginger, peeled
8 garlic cloves
6 green chiles
1 tablespoon whole black peppercorns
2 sprigs of curry leaves or 1 tablespoon
　crushed, dried curry leaves
2 tablespoons Madras curry powder (store-
　bought, or use our All-in-one Curry Powder,
　page 157)
1 teaspoon turmeric powder
5 tablespoons freshly squeezed lemon juice
2 eggs, beaten
2⅓ cup rice flour
½ teaspoon chile powder
½ teaspoon freshly ground black pepper
4 cups sunflower oil, for frying
sea salt, to taste, plus extra for sprinkling

1 Prep the chicken wings by scoring them on both sides (this will help them to cook much faster). Arrange in a wide, shallow dish.

2 In a blender, food processor, or mortar and pestle, blend or pound one of the pieces of ginger with the garlic, green chiles, whole black peppercorns, curry leaves, curry powder, and turmeric with the lemon juice and a pinch of salt to make a coarse paste. Coat the chicken wings in the paste and marinate for 2–3 hours in the refrigerator.

3 Meanwhile, slice the other piece of ginger into thin matchsticks and let sit.

4 When you're ready to cook, pour the beaten eggs over the marinated chicken wings and turn to coat well.

5 Tip the rice flour into a dish or onto a plate and stir in the chile powder and black pepper. Dredge the chicken wings through the flour, one by one, coating them thoroughly on all sides.

6 Heat the oil in a deep, heavy-bottomed pan over high heat to reach 325°F. Deep-fry the wings in small batches for 5–6 minutes until crispy and cooked. You can tell if they're cooked through by pricking the fattest part of the wing—the juices should run clear. If you're worried, finish them off on an oven preheated to 350°F for 10 minutes. After the chicken is fried, keep the oil hot and quickly drop in the ginger matchsticks. Cook for 1–2 minutes until crispy, then remove with a slotted spoon and drain on paper towels.

7 Serve the wings with your choice of dip (see pages 176–183), garnished with the crispy ginger and an extra sprinkling of salt.

# PICKLED SCALLOPS

## with WILD GARLIC AND CUMIN CAULIFLOWER

SERVES 2–4

Nirmal loves seafood, with scallops being a particular favorite. He's created a wonderful sauce to go with them here made with the springtime flush of wild garlic, but you can swap it out for chives when wild garlic is out of season.

FOR THE SCALLOPS
8 shelled sea scallops, rinsed and dried
1 teaspoon naga chile pickle
  (or any hot chile sauce)
sea salt, to taste

FOR THE WILD GARLIC CHUTNEY
3½ ounces wild garlic (or use chives when
  wild garlic is not in season)
1 ounce freshly chopped cilantro
½ teaspoon cumin seeds
2 garlic cloves
1 green chile, more or less, to taste
1 teaspoon freshly squeezed lime juice
1 tablespoon canola or olive oil

FOR THE CUMIN CAULIFLOWER
½ cauliflower head (approx. 3.5 ounces),
  broken into florets
3 tablespoons canola or olive oil
1 teaspoon cumin seeds
1 teaspoon freshly grated ginger
½ green chile, chopped
¼ teaspoon turmeric powder
1 tablespoon freshly squeezed lime juice

1 Place the scallops in a shallow dish with the naga chile pickle and a pinch of salt. Cover and leave to marinate in the refrigerator for 1 hour.

2 Place all the chutney ingredients in a blender and blend until smooth. Season with salt to taste and loosen with 1–2 tablespoons water, if necessary.

3 Blanch the cauliflower in a pot of boiling water for 2 minutes, then drain and refresh under cold water to prevent further cooking.

4 Heat the oil in a skillet over high heat and, once hot, add the cumin seeds, ginger, chile, and turmeric and stir together. Add the cauliflower and toss well to coat in the spices. Season with salt, to taste, and the lime juice and let sit.

5 Heat a non-stick skillet over high heat until just smoking and sear the scallops for 1 minute on each side until you see a golden brown crust.

6 Spread a little wild garlic chutney on each serving plate, top with the seared scallops and add a spoonful of the cumin cauliflower on the side.

# LOBSTER BALCHAO

SERVES 2

In India, if you want to escape for the holidays, Goa is the place to go. This dish is very much inspired by the cuisine of Goa and of memories of family holidays there.

2 raw lobster tails
1 tablespoon freshly squeezed lemon juice
½ teaspoon turmeric powder
4 dried red chiles
½ teaspoon black peppercorns
1 cinnamon stick
4 cloves
¼ cup malt vinegar
1 teaspoon freshly grated ginger
2 tablespoons canola or olive oil
1 onion, finely chopped
2 garlic cloves, finely minced
2 tomatoes, finely chopped
1 teaspoon jaggery or raw sugar
sea salt

1 To prepare the lobster tails, use a sharp knife or kitchen scissors to cut the tail lengthwise down from the center and remove any veins. Rinse well and pat dry.

2 Place the tails in a shallow dish with the lemon juice and turmeric. Season with salt and marinate in the refrigerator until you are ready to use.

3 In a spice or coffee grinder or mortar and pestle, finely grind the chiles, black peppercorns, cinnamon stick, and cloves to a powder. Mix with the malt vinegar, ginger, and a pinch of salt to make a paste.

4 Place a wide, heavy-bottomed pan over a high heat, then reduce the heat to medium and cook the onion for 5 minutes until soft and golden. Add the spice paste and cook for a minute until fragrant, then add the lobster and simmer, stirring continuously, for 5 minutes. Add the tomatoes and cook for 6–8 minutes until they break down and form a sauce, then stir through the jaggery and salt to balance the flavors. Check the lobster meat to ensure it's cooked through—to do this, insert a small knife into the center of the fattest part and pry it open. It should be white all the way through. Cook for a little longer if needed.

5 Serve warm. This is delicious with rice and a salad.

# MASALA FISH CAKES

MAKES 8 FISH CAKES

In Kolkata, we eat so much seafood, even to begin the day. In fact, my mum makes these for breakfast, and typically we'd eat them sandwiched between white bread—our take on a fish finger sandwich!

1 pound skinless whiting, cod or haddock, rinsed and dried
¼ teaspoon ground turmeric
a pinch of sea salt
1 pound floury potatoes, peeled and boiled
1 teaspoon freshly grated ginger
1 green chile, finely chopped
½ teaspoon cumin seeds, toasted and ground
3 tablespoons finely chopped cilantro
½ teaspoon freshly ground black pepper
½ teaspoon garam masala (store-bought, or see page 161)
2 eggs
1⅓ cup panko breadcrumbs
sunflower or canola oil, for shallow frying
your choice of dip (see pages 176–183), to serve

1 Place the fish in a wide, deep pot with a lid and sprinkle over the turmeric and salt. Pour in enough water to fully submerge, then cover and simmer over medium heat for 10 minutes. Strain and, once cooled, flake the fish onto a plate.

2 Grate the cooked potatoes into a bowl. Add the fish, ginger, chile, cumin, cilantro, black pepper, and garam masala and mix together well. Using your hands, shape the mixture into eight patties.

3 Whisk the eggs together in a shallow dish and place the panko breadcrumbs in a separate shallow dish.

4 Dip each fish cake in the beaten egg and then in the panko breadcrumbs, then repeat the process so that they are thoroughly coated. Refrigerate for 30 minutes (or pop in the freezer for 15 minutes).

5 Heat a shallow pool of oil in a non-stick skillet and, when hot, fry the fish cakes for about 4 minutes on each side, until golden and crisp. Add more oil to the pan, if necessary. Serve warm with your chosen dip.

# ETTI MASALA

## (SOUTH INDIAN-STYLE ShrimpS)

SERVES 2–4

Nirmal and I cemented our friendship over a few drinks—quite a few drinks, actually—and this is just the dish you need for such a drinking session. It's especially good with a cold glass of beer, but you could also make it as a generous garnish for the Malabar Shrimp Pulao (see page 123).

juice of 1 lime
1 tablespoon turmeric powder
1 tablespoon ground coriander
1 teaspoon crushed black pepper
12 jumbo shrimp
1 small onion, finely chopped
5 garlic cloves, finely minced
10 curry leaves (fresh are best if you can get them, but dried are fine), plus 6 extra leaves to garnish
1½ tablespoons coconut oil
1½ tablespoons canola oil
1 teaspoon green peppercorns, to garnish
a pinch of sea salt

1 In a bowl, mix together the lime juice, turmeric, ground coriander, black pepper, and a pinch of salt. Add the shrimp and turn to coat thoroughly, then cover and let sit to marinate for 15 minutes.

2 Heat the coconut oil in a non-stick skillet over high heat. Once melted, cook the onion with a pinch of salt for about 5 minutes until soft and lightly caramelised. Add the garlic and 10 of the curry leaves and cook for 2 minutes until golden.

3 Add the marinated shrimp and gently fry for 5 minutes until the mix is a little dry and the shrimps get a nice color on them. Remove the shrimp and keep warm. Quickly heat the canola oil in the hot pan and fry the remaining curry leaves until crispy.

4 Serve the shrimp hot, sprinkled with the green peppercorns and fried curry leaves.

# MUSSELS RASSA

You could say that this recipe is a fisherman's cheat, as it's rather simple and quick. The key is in using really fresh mussels so all their beautiful juices seep into the sauce. This is why we call it a fisherman's cheat—because the fisherman does most of the work!

4 tablespoons coconut oil
1 teaspoon yellow mustard seed
8 garlic cloves, finely sliced
1 thumb-sized piece of ginger, peeled and
   chopped into matchsticks
4 green chiles, halved lengthwise
10 curry leaves
1 small onion or 2 shallots, thinly sliced
1 teaspoon turmeric powder
1 teaspoon Madras curry powder (store-
   bought, or use our All-in-one Curry Powder,
   page 163)
½ teaspoon chile powder
1 cup fish stock
1¾ pound whole shelled mussels, rinsed,
   scrubbed, and drained (discard any that
   don't close in response to a tap)
½ cup coconut milk
a pinch of sugar
sea salt

TO SERVE
2 tablespoons finely chopped cilantro
½ lime
plain rice (optional)

1 Heat the oil in a large flameproof casserole pot with a lid, add the mustard seeds and wait for them to pop, then add the garlic, ginger, green chiles, and curry leaves and cook, stirring, for a minute.

2 Add the onion or shallots and gently cook for 5 minutes, then stir through the turmeric, curry and chile powders. Pour in the fish stock and cook over medium–high heat, stirring occasionally, until slightly reduced—about 15 minutes.

3 Add the cleaned mussels and coconut milk, stir and cover with the lid. Cook for 3–4 minutes until all the mussels have opened (discard any that remain closed), then season with the sugar (to balance the spices and heat) and salt, to taste.

4 Scatter with the chopped cilantro and serve the mussels hot on with a squeeze of lime, either on their own or with plain rice.

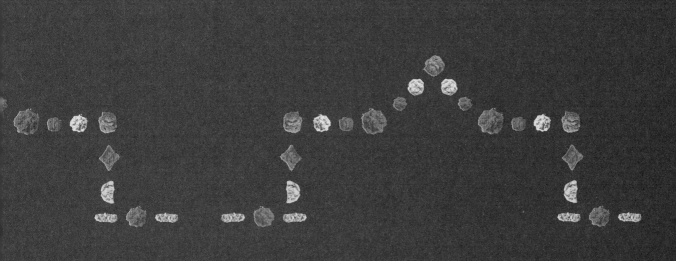

# BIG
# PLATES

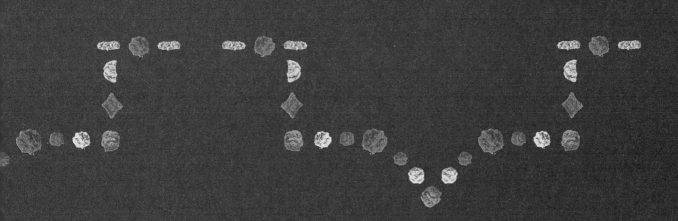

# BIG PLATES

Indian families are always massive and the best way to get everyone together is over a large homecooked meal. We show our love and affection through food, and dining together is when we connect the most. Typically, these gatherings of cousins, uncles, aunts, mothers, fathers, their children, and dear friends is as much about exchanging information—all the banter, gossip, opinions and news—as it is about sharing age-old recipes that have been handed down over many years, evolving with each new generation.

The following recipes are the ones we've harvested, shared, and grown. They're a collection of memories, delicious ones at that, and ones we hope you'll savor with those you cherish, too.

You don't need a celebration to make these dishes—the love and art of preparing them is a special occasion itself. The joy of these recipes is that they make larger portions that can be served communally. If you're lucky, you'll end up with leftovers, so you can keep feasting as the week rolls on.

# ACHARI PARTRIDGE

## with PICKLED YOGURT DIP and ROASTED PINEAPPLE SALAD

SERVES 4

This is a famous recipe in the south west of India, where game dishes are very popular. The first marinade is almost like a pickle—it gives the meat so much flavor and renders it so tender before it hits the grill.

2 red partridge legs, cut in
 half lengthwise

FOR THE FIRST MARINADE
4 tablespoons freshly squeezed
 lemon juice
2 teaspoons freshly grated ginger
2 garlic cloves, finely minced
½ teaspoon chile powder
1 teaspoon sea salt

FOR THE SECOND MARINADE
¾ cup Greek yogurt
5 tablespoons lime pickle
1 tablespoon freshly grated ginger
1 green chile, finely chopped
1 teaspoon dried fenugreek leaves
1 teaspoon nigella seeds
3 tablespoons mustard or
 canola oil
½ teaspoon chile powder, to taste
sea salt, to taste

FOR THE ROASTED PINEAPPLE SALAD
1 pineapple, peeled, cored, and cut
 into ¾-inch-thick slices
2 tablespoons honey
2 teaspoons chaat masala
1 teaspoon freshly ground black
 pepper
1 teaspoon superfine sugar
4 scallions, finely chopped
1 green chile, finely chopped

FOR THE PICKLED YOGURT DIP
1 cup Greek yogurt
1 teaspoon naga chile pickle, to
 taste
½ teaspoon superfine sugar

1  In a large bowl, mix together all the ingredients for the first marinade. Toss the partridge in the mixture until thoroughly coated, then cover and let sit to marinate for 30 minutes.

2  In a separate bowl, mix together the ingredients for the second marinade, then pour over the marinating partridge and stir to coat. Cover and refrigerate for 3 hours, or overnight.

3  Preheat your oven broiler to high. In a bowl, mix the pineapple slices with the honey, chaat masala, black pepper, and sugar and then let sit to marinate for 15 minutes. Arrange the pineapple slices on a baking sheet in a single layer. Broil for 5–10 minutes on each side or until each side is nicely colored. Let sit to cool, then chop into small dice and mix with the scallion and green chile. Refrigerate until ready to eat.

4  In a small bowl, mix together all the ingredients for the pickled yogurt dip.

5  When you're ready to cook, preheat your oven broiler to high. Arrange the partridge in a shallow ovenproof dish and broil for 10 minutes on each side until cooked through. Test by piercing the fattest part of the meat with a skewer or sharp knife. The juices should be clear. If not, cook for a little longer.

6  Serve hot with the pickled yogurt dip and roasted pineapple salad on the side.

# GHEE ROAST PEPPER QUAIL
## with GUNPOWDER DOSA

SERVES 4

Nirmal is a master when it comes to preparing game dishes. These are all recipes inspired by his home village, where game is eaten far more often than chicken. The dosa can be paired with lots of other recipes in the book, such as the Market-style Scrambled Eggs (see page 20). This recipe requires overnight marinating and fermenting. *Pictured on pages 84–85.*

4 whole quails, butterflied (you can ask your butcher to do this)
3 tablespoons ghee
12 fresh curry leaves
2 onions, finely chopped
2 garlic cloves, finely chopped
2 teaspoons freshly ground black pepper

FOR THE MARINADE
3 tablespoons freshly squeezed lemon juice
2 teaspoons freshly grated ginger
2 garlic cloves, finely minced
1 green chile, finely chopped
2 teaspoons garam masala (store-bought, or see page 161)
1 teaspoon freshly ground black pepper
½ teaspoon turmeric powder
½ teaspoon red chile powder, to taste
1 drop of cinnamon essential oil or ½ teaspoon ground cinnamon
sea salt, to taste

FOR THE DOSA
¾ cup urad dal flour (see Tip)
1¼ cup rice flour
1 teaspoon sea salt
2¼ cups filtered or mineral water
3–4 tablespoons canola oil
1 tablespoon Gunpowder Spice Mix (see page 158)

1  In a large bowl, mix together all the ingredients for the marinade. Add the quails and toss to coat well, then marinate for 4 hours or overnight in the refrigerator.

2  To make the dosa, mix together the flours and salt in a bowl and, little by little, add the filtered or mineral water to make a thick batter. Keep mixing as you add the water and stop when the batter is the consistency of heavy cream.

3  Cover the batter and let sit in a warm place to ferment for 8 hours or overnight. It should be quite bubbly and airy once it's fermented. However, it might also have thickened, so before cooking you may need to add a little more water to return it to the consistency of heavy cream.

4  Place a large skillet over high heat and add enough oil to gloss the surface of the pan. Add 2–3 tablespoons of dosa batter, swirl around the base to coat evenly, and cook both sides until golden brown. Sprinkle a pinch of gunpowder spice over the cooked dosa and remove from the pan. Continue until you've used up all the batter (you should get about eight dosa). Let sit.

5  Place the quail and all of the marinade in a large lidded flameproof casserole pot over medium heat. Pop the lid on snugly, reduce the heat and cook until the quail is tender, about 30–35 minutes. If there is liquid left, cook on a slightly higher heat to evaporate it. Once cooked, let sit with the lid still on for 30 minutes to rest.

6  Place a large skillet over medium heat. When hot, add the ghee and fry the curry leaves until crisp, then remove and reserve. Add the onion and garlic to the pan and cook, stirring, for 5 minutes until soft and a little golden. Add the quails along with any marinade and sprinkle over the black pepper. Fry for 5–10 minutes until all the pepper, quail, ghee, and cinnamon aromas are released, then take off the heat.

7  Garnish with the crispy curry leaves and serve hot with the dosa.

TIP

If you have a spice or coffee grinder, you can make your own urad dal flour by simply grinding urad dal lentils to a fine powder.

BIG PLATES

86

# PHEASANT BHUJING PULAO

SERVES 2–4

Nirmal's mother makes this wonderful dish—it's a family favorite. It's incredibly comforting and unusual in that it uses rice flakes, making it rather like a savory porridge. But you can easily make it more biryani-like by using cooked white or brown basmati rice instead.

1 whole pheasant, skinned and cut into
   8 pieces
6 baby potatoes, peeled and sliced into
   ½ inch-thick rounds
3 tablespoons canola or olive oil
6 cloves
1 cinnamon stick
6 black peppercorns
4 green cardamom
2 onions, finely chopped
1 teaspoon turmeric powder
A pinch of chile powder
1 teaspoon ground cumin
1 teaspoon ground coriander
1 teaspoon garam masala (store-bought,
   or see page 161)
8½ ounces medium-sized rice flakes
sea salt, to taste

FOR THE MARINADE
5 tablespoons Greek yogurt
2 ounces freshly chopped cilantro
10 mint leaves
1 green chile
3 garlic cloves, finely minced
1 tablespoon freshly grated ginger

TO SERVE
chopped fresh cilantro
freshly squeezed lime juice
your choice of Raita (see pages 176–183)

1  For a superior, smoky flavor, prepare a charcoal barbecue. If you don't have one, preheat your oven broiler to high.

2  Blitz the marinade ingredients together in a food processor or mortar and pestle to make a thick paste. Rub half the paste into the pheasant pieces and baby potatoes and leave to marinate for 30 minutes. Reserve the rest.

3  On the barbecue or under the broiler, broil the marinated pheasant pieces for about 10 minutes, turning once or twice. Parboil the sliced potatoes in a pan with just enough salted water to cover them for about 10 minutes, until just tender.

4  Meanwhile, set a large pot with a lid over medium heat. Add the oil and, once hot, add the cloves, cinnamon, peppercorns, and cardamom pods, followed by the onions. Gently fry until golden—about 10 minutes.

5  Fold through the remaining spices, the rest of the green paste, a pinch of salt and 1 cup water. Cover and cook for 10 minutes.

6  Fold the broiled pheasant and potatoes through the sauce and cook for 10 minutes.

7  Add the rice and check that the quantity of sauce is just enough to soak the rice flakes— if not, top up with enough water to cover by ¾. Simmer just long enough to soften the rice flakes, and take off the heat. Stir in the fresh cilantro and a squeeze lime, to taste. Serve with your choice of Raita.

TIP

Rice flakes (*poha*) go dry after a while, so serve immediately. If you can't find rice flakes, you can swap them out with cooked basmati rice.

# MALVANI SUKKA CHICKEN

SERVES 4

Malvan is a coastal area in Konkan, which has its own distinct way of cooking food. The region's cuisine is famous for using coconut liberally. Dried red chiles and cardamom are also dominant features in local dishes. The sauce for this gorgeous chicken is so beautiful—it's lovely served with rice or dosas (see page 86) to help mop it all up.

8 chicken drumsticks
4 whole dried kashmiri red chiles
2 teaspoons coriander seeds
½ teaspoon black peppercorns
4 cloves
½ teaspoon cumin seeds
seeds from 5 green cardamom pods
seeds from 2 black cardamom pods
1 tablespoon dried coconut
1 teaspoon poppy seeds
2 teaspoons fennel seeds
2 star anise
½ cinnamon stick
4 tablespoons canola or coconut oil
2 large onions, finely chopped
a handful of freshly chopped cilantro,
   to garnish
sea salt

1  Score the chicken drumsticks by piercing them all over with the tip of a sharp knife; this will help them cook faster and absorb all the flavors from the sauce.

2  Place a skillet over medium heat and dry-roast the chiles for a minute., then Let sit.

3  In the same pan, dry-roast the coriander seeds, cloves, black peppercorns, cumin seeds, green and black cardamom seeds, desiccated coconut, poppy seeds, fennel seeds, star anise, and cinnamon for 1–2 minutes until all their aromas are released. Let sit to cool.

4  Combine the spices in a mortar and pestle or spice grinder and grind to a powder. For extra heat, grind the dry-roasted chiles, too, or add them to the dish whole for a milder heat. Transfer the ground spices to a bowl and whisk in ¾ cup warm water to create a smooth paste. Let sit.

5  Heat the oil in a sauté pan over medium heat. Add the onions and a pinch of salt and cook for 4 minutes. Stir in the prepared spice paste (and the whole chiles if you didn't grind them) and cook for 15 seconds.

6  Add the chicken drumsticks with ½ cup water and stir well to incorporate. Cook for 30 minutes, stirring occasionally. Once you see oil starting to release from the sides of the sauce, turn off the heat.

7  Garnish with chopped cilantro and serve the chicken hot with the sauce spooned over the top.

# ORGANIC TANDOORI CHICKEN

SERVES 4

Every Indian boy worth his salt likes a good tandoori chicken. Of course, every family has their own take on the iconic dish, but we have to say ours is pretty special. The fenugreek and mango powder give it that magic touch.

3 pounds organic chicken or 4 chicken legs
2 garlic cloves, finely chopped
1 tablespoon freshly grated ginger
1 green chile, finely chopped
3 tablespoons freshly squeezed lime juice
1 tablespoon mustard or canola oil
3 tablespoons Greek yogurt
3 tablespoons finely chopped cilantro
1 tablespoon smoked paprika
½ tablespoon mango powder
½ tablespoon garam masala (store-bought, or see page 161)
½ tablespoon dried fenugreek leaves
1 tablespoon ground coriander
½ tablespoon ground cumin
4 tablespoons Kashmiri chile oil (see Tip)

1 If you're using a whole chicken, remove the giblets (if it has them). Using a large, sharp knife, cut down through the breastbone of the chicken, prise the bird open and cut down through the backbone so that the chicken is in two identical halves—each with a breast, leg, and wing. Alternatively, you can just use four chicken legs.

2 Pull the skin off the chicken and, using a knife again, score the fatter parts of the chicken legs and breast as this will help them cook faster and absorb all the flavors from the marinade.

3 In a bowl, mix together the garlic, ginger, and chile with the lime juice and mustard or rapeseed oil. Use your hands to rub this all over the chicken, then let sit for 10 minutes.

4 In a separate bowl, mix together all the remaining ingredients to form a paste, then rub this all over the chicken, too. Cover and marinate for 30 minutes (or you can leave it in the refrigerator overnight).

5 Prepare a charcoal barbecue or preheat your oven to 425°F. If using a barbecue, thread the marinated chicken onto skewers and turn regularly to cook all sides evenly. This should take about 15–20 minutes. Alternatively, arrange the chicken on a broiling pan and cook in the oven for about 40 minutes or until nicely charred all over and cooked all the way through—you can test by piercing the fattest part of the chicken and seeing if the juices run clear—if not, cook a little longer. Rest for 20 minutes before serving.

6 Serve with Bhurani raita (see page 176) and salad.

TIP

To make your own Kashmiri chile oil, simply infuse two broken Kashmiri chiles in a bottle with 1 cup olive or canola oil for two weeks. For a faster infusion, heat the oil, add the chiles and gently warm for 15 minutes, then infuse for an additional15 minutes and strain.

# DUM-PUKTH CHICKEN

SERVES 4

Dum is a very special way of cooking meat or fish from northern India. The *dum* refers to sealing the pot with a simple flour, salt, and water-based dough. The seal locks in the moisture and lets the meat or fish steam in its own juices. This dish has a large amount of fenugreek leaves—you can use dried or fresh. They're incredibly good for you, especially for your digestion. My wife and I eat this dish a lot at home.

8 chicken thighs
1 tablespoon freshly grated ginger
8 garlic cloves, finely chopped
1–2 green chiles, finely chopped
6 tablespoons freshly chopped
    cilantro, plus extra to garnish
3 tablespoons ghee
1 onion, finely chopped
3 tablespoons Greek yogurt
2 bay leaves
½ cup fenugreek leaves
1 teaspoon ground cumin
1 teaspoon ground coriander
½ teaspoon ground mace
ground seeds from 16 green
    cardamom pods
fresh cilantro, to garnish
sea salt

FOR THE DOUGH (FOR SEALING THE POT)
2 cups all-purpose flour
3 tablespoons olive or canola oil

1 Using a sharp knife, score each chicken thigh about ½ inch deep at ¾–1¼ inch intervals, as this will help the meat absorb all the flavors from the dish.

2 In a bowl, mix together the ginger, garlic, green chile, and half the fresh cilantro to make a paste.

3 Place a sauté pan over medium heat, add half the ghee and, once melted, cook the onion with a pinch of salt until it's nicely golden. Transfer to a blender and blend to make a fine paste, then stir into the ginger paste and whisk in the yogurt. Slather this marinade over the chicken, cover and marinate in the refrigerator for 6 hours or overnight.

4 Remove the chicken from the refrigerator and bring up to room temperature before using.

5 For the dough, mix together the flour, ½ cup water and the oil in a bowl until the mixture resembles uncooked pastry. Add a little more flour or water if necessary.

6 Place a flameproof casserole pot with a lid over medium heat. Add the remaining ghee, together with the bay leaves and marinated chicken and cook until it starts to brown a little all over.

7 Add the fenugreek leaves with the cumin and ground coriander and stir well. The heap of fenugreek will make it look a little dry, but once you cover the pot, the steam inside will keep everything tender and moist.

8 Cover the dish with the lid and seal using the dough. Cook over low heat for 35 minutes until the chicken is cooked through and the flavors are all released.

9 Sprinkle the chicken with the ground mace and cardamom and serve hot garnished with chopped cilantro. This is delicious with salad and rice.

# GOAN PORK

SERVES 2–4

In Goa, they eat pork because the region is predominantly Christian. Of course, in Muslim regions of India, pork does not feature. At Gunpowder, Nirmal favors pork from Gloucestershire Old Spots, a heritage breed. The use of vinegar in this dish is very traditional. Dishes like 'vin'-daloo reference the use of vinegar, which really balances the flavors.

1 pound diced pork
5 tablespoons canola or olive oil
2 onions, finely chopped
1 tablespoon freshly grated ginger
3 garlic cloves, finely minced
2 whole dried red chiles
5 tablespoons red wine vinegar
cooked red Goan rice, to serve (available online, in Indian stores and in larger grocery stores)
sea salt

FOR THE MARINADE
1 tablespoon coriander seeds
1 teaspoon cumin seeds
½ teaspoon black peppercorns
1 cinnamon stick
3 cloves
1 teaspoon freshly grated ginger
2 garlic cloves, peeled
1 teaspoon turmeric powder
1 teaspoon brown sugar
1 teaspoon yellow mustard seed
½ teaspoon fenugreek seeds

1 Begin with the marinade. Place a skillet over medium heat and toast all the whole spices for the marinade for 1–2 minutes or until fragrant. Leave to cool a little, then transfer them to a mortar and pestle or spice grinder. Grind them to a fine powder, then mix with the other marinade ingredients. Rub the mixture into the pork all over, cover and marinate in the refrigerator for 4 hours, or overnight.

2 When you're ready to cook, heat the oil in a sauté pan with a lid over medium heat. Once hot, stir in the onions with a pinch of salt and gently fry for about 5 minutes until golden. Add the ginger and garlic and cook for 30 seconds, then add the marinated pork, along with the dried chiles and vinegar.

3 Fry the pork for 10 minutes until a little golden on each side, then add 1 cup water and bring to the boil. Reduce the heat, cover with the lid and cook for 45 minutes until the meat is tender.

4 Serve with red Goan rice.

# WILD RABBIT PULAO

SERVES 4–6

We call this Aunty Sulu's pulao. It comes from Nirmal's mother. She made this for me after Nirmal and his wife had their first child. I brought a gift to the house and in exchange she asked me what I'd like her to cook for me. I'd tried her famous rabbit pulao before, so this was the dish I requested.

1 whole wild rabbit (around 2 pounds), prepared and cut into 5–6 pieces
1½ cups long grain basmati rice
½ cup dried cranberries or sour cherries
4 tablespoons olive or canola oil
3 tablespoons ghee
2 onions, thinly sliced
1 cup vegetable stock
6 green cardamom pods
8 cloves
1 cinnamon stick
1 bay leaf
12 strands of saffron, soaked in 3 tablespoons warm water for 10 minutes to release the color and aroma
3 tablespoons freshly squeezed lemon juice
1 cup freshly chopped mint leaves, to garnish
1 ounce freshly chopped cilantro, to garnish
sea salt

FOR THE MARINADE
3 tablespoons freshly grated ginger
4 garlic cloves, finely minced
5 tablespoons natural yogurt
1 green chile, finely chopped
a pinch of chile powder
1 tablespoon turmeric powder
6 tablespoons finely chopped mint leaves
6 tablespoons freshly chopped cilantro
3 tablespoons garam masala (store-bought, or see page 161)

1  Check over the rabbit and remove any shot remnants you might find (they'll be little lead dots the size of a coriander seed or smaller).

2  In a large bowl, mix together all the marinade ingredients and then use your hands to rub the mixture into the meat. Cover and marinate in the refrigerator for 6 hours, or overnight. Bring up to room temperature before using.

3  Place the rice in a dish, cover with water and soak for 30 minutes. Place the cranberries or cherries in a separate dish and cover with water. Add a pinch of salt.

4  Heat 2 tablespoons of the oil and the ghee in a sauté pan with a lid over medium heat. Stir in the onion with a large pinch of salt, as this will help draw the moisture from the onion and speed up the cooking. Sauté for 5 minutes until dark brown.

5  Add the rabbit with all the marinade and cook until nicely colored all over. Pour in the vegetable stock and stir well, then cover with the lid. Reduce the heat and simmer gently for 1 hour.

6  In the meantime, pour 2½ cups water into a large saucepan. Add the cardamom, cloves, cinnamon, and bay and bring to the boil over medium heat. Reduce the heat, cover with a lid and simmer for 15 minutes or so until all the flavors from the whole spices infuse the water. Add the remaining oil and ½ teaspoon salt, then drain your soaking rice and add to the boiling water. Cook for 12 minutes or until all the water has been absorbed. Take off the heat but keep the lid on to let it steam through for an additional 5 minutes.

7  Check that the rabbit is tender, then take off the heat and mix with the rice. Strain the cranberries or cherries and stir through the dish together with the saffron, soaking water and all. Season with salt, to taste, and finish with the lemon juice and freshly chopped mint and cilantro.

# KOSBADI RABBIT MASALA

This is another famous rabbit dish from Nirmal's mother, nicknamed Aunty Sulu. The recipe gets its name from Kosbad, which is a village in the Palghar district of Maharashtra.

3 tablespoons canola or
　coconut oil
4 cloves
½ cinnamon stick
1 onion, finely chopped
¼ teaspoon turmeric powder
1 tomato, finely chopped
4 rabbit legs, each leg cut into
　3 pieces (see Tip), rinsed and
　dried

FOR THE SPICE PASTE
3–4 dried Kashmiri red chiles
2 teaspoons coriander seeds
1 teaspoon cumin seeds
1 teaspoon black peppercorns
4 garlic cloves, finely minced
1 tablespoon, freshly grated ginger
3 tablespoons natural yogurt

TO GARNISH AND TO SERVE
½ cup canola or sunflower oil
1 small onion or shallot, thinly sliced
a thumb-sized piece of ginger,
　peeled and cut into julienne strips
a handful of mint leaves, finely
　chopped
lemon wedges

1  Place a skillet over high heat. Add the chiles and cook for 30 seconds. Reduce the heat to medium, add the coriander seeds, cumin seeds and peppercorns and toast for 2 minutes until fragrant, then leave to cool a little. Transfer to a spice grinder or mortar and pestle and grind to a fine powder. Place in a bowl with the garlic, ginger, and yogurt and mix together to make a paste.

2  Heat the oil in a flameproof casserole pot with a lid over high heat. Once hot, stir in the cloves and cinnamon and fry until aromatic, then fold in the onion and cook for 5 minutes until golden.

3  Add the turmeric and tomato and cook for 5–10 minutes until the tomato has broken down and darkened a little.

4  Add the rabbit and fry for 3–4 minutes, then add ⅔ cup water and a pinch of salt. Stir well to incorporate, then cover with the lid and cook for an additional 5–6 minutes.

5  Remove the lid, stir in the ground spice paste and cook for a few more minutes until the sauce has been absorbed and the rabbit is tender but cooked through—it should be starting to pull away from the bone. Season with a little more salt, to taste.

6  For the garnishes, heat the oil in a small, deep pot until bubbling hot, then add the onion or shallot and cook until golden. Remove with a slotted spoon and drain on paper towels. Add the ginger to the hot oil and fry until golden, then drain on paper towels and dust with a little salt.

7  Serve the rabbit sprinkled with the fried onion, crispy ginger, and fresh mint leaves, and with lemon wedges on the side.

## TIP

You can easily cut through the bones of the rabbit with a sharp cook's knife or bread knife, or you can ask you butcher to do this for you. You could also swap the four legs used here for a whole rabbit, cut into 5–6 pieces.

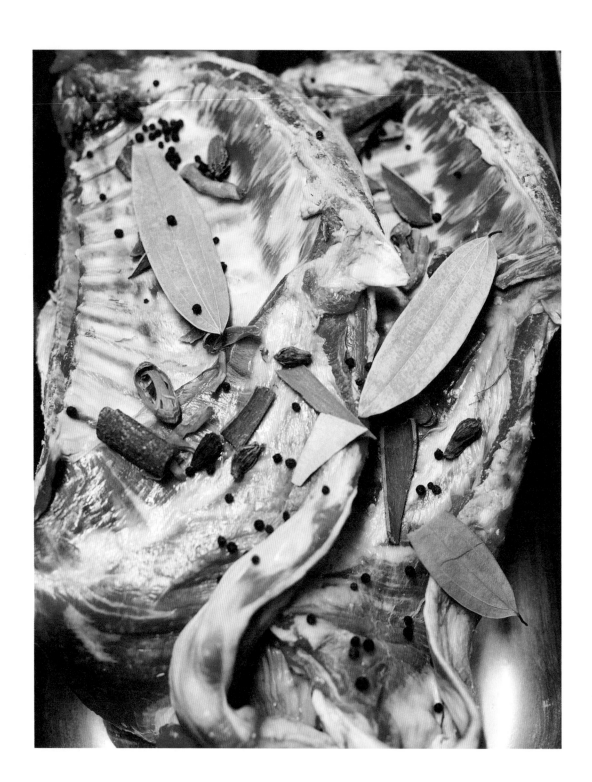

# KOLHAPURI LAMB SHANKS

SERVES 4

If you have friends coming over for dinner, this is a wonderful dish to make. It comes from Nirmal's village. It's a slow-cooking dish, so it takes a while, but it's easy—once you put it in the pot, you don't have to do anything, just let it simmer away until the meat falls apart. If you're lucky enough to have leftovers the next day, shred the meat, sandwich it between two slices of white bread, add a little mustard inside and fry the sandwich in butter—or brush the outside with mayo and grill it (this sounds odd, but it creates the most wonderful crust). Leftovers are also wonderful fried with rice.

3 tablespoons coconut or canola oil
2 onions, finely chopped
1 teaspoon turmeric powder
½ teaspoon asafoetida
1 tablespoon freshly grated ginger
3 garlic cloves, finely chopped
2 tomatoes, finely diced
4 (½ pound) lamb shanks, excess fat trimmed
3 tablespoons deggi mirch spice blend (see Note)
2 teaspoons yellow chile powder (see Note)
1 tablespoon garam masala (store-bought, or see page 161)
4 cups vegetable or lamb stock
1 cup grated fresh coconut (see page 51)
2 teaspoons sesame seeds
2 teaspoons poppy seeds
a thumb-sized piece of ginger, peeled and julienned, to serve
freshly chopped cilantro, to serve
sea salt

1  Heat the oil in a flameproof casserole pot with a lid over medium heat and cook the onions for 5 minutes until translucent.
Stir in the turmeric, asafoetida, ginger, garlic, and tomatoes and sizzle, stirring often, for 10 minutes or until the tomatoes have broken down into a thick sauce.

2  Add the lamb shanks and sauté for 5 minutes and until coated all over in the thickened sauce. Stir in the deggi mirch, yellow chile powder, garam masala, and a pinch of salt and then add the stock. Bring to the boil, then reduce the heat and cover with a lid.

3  Place a skillet over medium heat and gently dry-roast the coconut for 2 minutes until just golden. Transfer to a blender or food processor with the sesame and poppy seeds and blend to a paste.

4  Stir the paste into the lamb shank sauce, then replace the lid and continue to cook, stirring occasionally, over low heat for 3 hours or until the lamb is so tender that it easily falls off the bone.

5  Serve the lamb in a dish with the sauce spooned on top and finish with fine matchsticks of fresh ginger and a scattering of freshly chopped cilantro.

## NOTES

Deggi mirch is a full-flavored Indian chile powder that's relatively mild in heat. It is slightly hotter than paprika but is used more to add color than heat to dishes. Paprika measures about 500 Scoville Heat Units (SHU) on the Scoville scale, while deggi mirch is around 1,500 to 2,000 SHU and cayenne chile pepper can measure anything up to 50,000 SHU. When dry, deggi mirch can taste similar to paprika, but when it is fried in oil, the spice blooms to give more heat and adds a different flavor to the dish. That said, you can swap the deggi mirch for 2 tablespoons paprika and 1 tablespoon cayenne pepper.

The yellow chile powder is difficult to substitute. Both can be found online or in specialist Indian supermarkets and stores, but if you can't find it, just add more paprika in its place.

# JACKFRUIT AND GUCCHI PULAO

SERVES 4–6

My grandfather used to send my mother parcels of exotic ingredients from his travels. He was a real foodie and *gucchi*, which means dried morel mushrooms, is one thing my mother loved receiving in his edible parcels. My mother is vegetarian, so ingredients like mushrooms and jackfruit—a wonderful substitute for meat—are ones she cooks with often. In India, we treat jackfruit like pulled lamb. It's beautiful in this dish.

⅓ cup ghee
2 bay leaves
1 cinnamon stick, broken in half
6 cloves
4 green cardamom pods, bruised
2 teaspoons black cumin seeds (see Tip)
2 onions, thinly sliced
1½ cups basmati rice, rinsed and drained
1¾ ounces dried morel or porcini mushrooms
5 ounces canned jackfruit (drained weight), shredded into smaller pieces
a good pinch of saffron (about 10 strands), soaked in 1–2 tablespoons water for about 10 minutes to release colour and aroma
½ cup sunflower or canola oil
sea salt

1 Heat the ghee in a flameproof casserole pot with a lid. Add the bay leaves, broken cinnamon stick, cloves, bruised cardamom pods, and cumin seeds and fry for 30 seconds until fragrant.

2 Add one of the sliced onions and sauté for 5 minutes until it caramelizes slightly, then add the drained rice and a good pinch of salt. Fry for a minute, then add the mushrooms, jackfruit and 1¾ cups water.

3 When the rice mixture comes to the boil, reduce the heat, add the saffron, cover with a lid and cook for 12–15 minutes until the rice is done and the water is absorbed. Take off the heat but keep the lid on to allow the rice to steam through.

4 In a small pot, heat the oil until bubbling, then drop in the remaining onion slices and fry for 5 minutes over fairly high heat until just golden and crisp. Remove with a slotted spoon, drain on paper towels and sprinkle with salt. Serve the rice with the crispy onions scattered over the top.

TIP
Use normal cumin seeds if you can't find black cumin.

# MAA'S KASHMIRI LAMB CHOPS

SERVES 4

The "Maa" referred to in this recipe, which has to be one of the most popular dishes on our menu, is my wife Devina's mother. She made this for me when we first met. This recipe shows you how to make the dish using a whole rack of lamb, which makes an impressive center piece, but if you prefer you can make it with lamb cutlets instead, as we do in the restaurant.

8-bone rack of lamb,
    French-trimmed
3 tablespoons freshly squeezed
    lime juice
1 teaspoon chile powder
1 teaspoon mango powder (see
    Note)
½ teaspoon freshly grated nutmeg
1 teaspoon freshly ground black
    pepper
½ teaspoon fenugreek seeds
sea salt

TO SERVE
lemon wedges
1 tablespoon Gunpowder
    spice blend (see page 158)
Kashmiri Radish and Beet Pickle (see
    page 168)

FOR THE MARINADE
¾-inch piece of fresh ginger, peeled
4 garlic cloves, peeled
½ green chile
1 tablespoon mustard or canola oil
½ teaspoon fennel seeds
¼ teaspoon ground cinnamon
½ cup heavy cream

FOR THE CHUTNEY
2 tablespoons mint chutney
1 ounce chopped fresh cilantro
4 tablespoons Greek yogurt
2 teaspoons superfine sugar
1 green chile
2 garlic cloves, very finely chopped
2 teaspoons cumin seeds,
    toasted and ground
½ teaspoon mango powder
    (see Note)
4 tablespoons freshly squeezed
    lemon juice
sea salt, to taste

1  First make the marinade. Place the ginger, garlic, green chile, and oil in a blender or food processor and pulse until coarsely chopped. Transfer to a bowl, add the fennel seeds, cinnamon, and heavy cream and stir to mix well.

2  Place the rack of lamb in a shallow, ovenproof dish and spoon over the creamy marinade to coat thoroughly. Marinate in the refrigerator for 3–4 hours before cooking.

3  To make the chutney, place all the ingredients in a blender or food processor and blend until you have a smooth, pale green mixture. Cover and chill until ready to serve. (It will keep for 3–4 days in the refrigerator.)

4  In a bowl, mix the lime juice, chile powder, mango powder, nutmeg, black pepper, fenugreek, and a pinch of salt. Turn the marinated lamb rack through the mix to coat.

5  Preheat your oven to 400°F. Place the lamb on a baking sheet, fat side up. Roast for 15–17 minutes if you like it rare, or leave for 4–5 minutes longer if you prefer if more well done. Remove from the oven, cover, and leave to rest for at least 10 minutes.

6  Carve the rack between the bones into chops. Serve with a squeeze of lemon, a dusting of Gunpowder spice, and a little pot of the chutney on the side, as well as some pickled radishes.

## NOTE

You can buy mango powder (also called amchoor) in specialist Indian stores.
It's made from tart green mangos and has a lemony flavor similar to sumac.
Use sumac or lime zest if you can't find it.

# ANDHRA STYLE GREY MULLET

I used to work for my dad's company as a travelling salesman. Earlier in the book, I mentioned the work canteens we would stop by for food. Who knew they'd inspire so many recipes? On the whole, the canteens were quite basic. You paid just a few rupees for the basics of rice, lentils and salad, but what made the meal exciting was getting to choose a main course to go along with it. We were in Andhra when I tried a dish very similar to this one, and I never forgot it.

FOR THE MARINADE
4 grey mullet fillets
   (approx. 7 ounces each)
1 teaspoon freshly ground black
   pepper
1 tablespoon freshly grated ginger
1 tablespoon freshly squeezed
   lemon juice

FOR THE ANDHRA SAUCE
3 tablespoons canola oil
2 teaspoon yellow mustard seeds
2 teaspoon cumin seeds
¼ teaspoon fenugreek seeds
¼ teaspoon asafoetida
12 curry leaves
1 large onion, finely chopped
2 large tomatoes, finely chopped
1 tablespoon ground coriander
1 tablespoon kashmiri chile powder
   (see Note)
1½ teaspoon turmeric powder
1 teaspoon tamarind paste
2¼ cups coconut cream

FOR FRYING THE FISH
3 tablespoons canola oil

1 Rinse the fish, pat dry, and lay in a shallow dish. Whisk the black pepper, ginger, lemon juice, and a good pinch of salt together. Pour the mix over the fish and let sit to marinate for 10 minutes.

2 In the meantime, set a pot with a lid over medium heat. Add the oil for the sauce and, once hot, stir in the mustard seeds followed by cumin seeds and fenugreek seeds. When the mustard seeds start to crackle, add the asafoetida and curry leaves. Fry, stirring, for 30 seconds.

3 Fold the onion through the oil and spices and sauté for 10 minutes, or until it becomes translucent. Add the tomato, coriander, chile powder, turmeric, and 1 cup water. Stir well, then cover with a lid and simmer over medium heat for 10–15 minutes, or until the tomato has fully cooked down.

4 Remove the lid, add the tamarind pulp and mix it in well. Let it cook for a minute, then whisk in the coconut cream and cook for an additionalminute. Season with salt, turn off the heat and keep the sauce ready to serve.

5 Set a skillet over high heat to fry the fish. Add the oil and then the marinated fish, skin-side down. Fry for 3–5 minutes or until the skin is golden and crisp. Turn the fish over and cook for 2–3 minutes, or until it is just cooked through.

6 Spoon the sauce onto a large platter or serving plates and perch the fish on top, crispy skin-side up. This is delicious when garnished with crispy leeks.

## NOTE

Kashmiri chiles are quite mild and have a rich, fruity taste. You can buy large bags of dried Kashmiri chiles in Indian supermarkets or online. Turn them into a chile powder by grinding them in a coffee or spice grinder. If you can't find Kashmiri chiles or Kashmiri chile powder, use normal chile powder but halve the quantity.

# PATURI MACCH

Mustard seeds feature a lot in dishes from my home city, Kolkata. They are a really healthy spice and in this dish their heat is mellowed by the addition of fresh coconut. This nutritious dish is perfect for the barbecue, especially if you prefer fish to meat—just skip the steaming step and place the wrapped fish on the barbecue. It might take a little longer to cook through because you're not steaming it first.

1 pound 3 ounces skinless cod fillet, cut into 4 equal-sized pieces
4 (9-inch) square banana leaf (see tip)

FOR THE MARINADE
1 cup whole grain mustard
3 tablespoons mustard or canola oil
5 tablespoons freshly squeezed lemon juice
5 tablespoons grated fresh coconut (see page 51) or dried coconut
3 tablespoons freshly grated ginger
4 garlic cloves, finely minced
1 green chile, finely chopped
1 teaspoon Kashmiri chile powder (see Note opposite)
2 tablespoons turmeric powder
1 fish or vegetable stock cube, crumbled

1  In a bowl, mix together all the marinade ingredients to a make a coarse paste.

2  Lay the fish pieces on a plate and cover with the paste until thoroughly and evenly coated. Cover and marinate in the refrigerator for 2–3 hours.

3  Gently warm the banana leaves over a gas flame on the stovetop for 10–20 seconds on each side, ensuring that they don't burn.

4  Place each marinated fish piece in the center of a banana leaf square and fold the leaf over like an envelope (you can tie it together with kitchen string).

5  Transfer the fish parcels to a steamer basket and steam for 25 minutes. Alternatively, gently heat 3 tablespoons water in a skillet with a lid, then add the parcels, cover with the lid and steam them that way.

6  Place a dry grill pan over high heat and grill each fish parcel for 2 minutes on each side until it is charred with the grill marks. Serve hot. This fish is lovely with rice and the Okra Raita with Pomegranate on page 180.

## TIP

If you don't have any banana leaves, you can use any other edible leaf, such as a large fig leaf or wine (grape) leaves, or simply use foil or parchment paper.

# DUM-KI-MACHLI

SERVES 4

Nirmal's face lights up when you mention this dish. He loves it so much that every time I visit him in his village he makes it for me. What makes this recipe unique is the little parcel of smouldering charcoal, which gives the dish a smoky edge as it cooks.

4 tablespoons ghee, plus ½ teaspoon for the charcoal
4 onions, thinly sliced
4 tablespoons freshly squeezed lemon juice
2 teaspoons ginger, peeled and finely grated
1 large garlic clove, finely minced
1 teaspoon garam masala (store-bought, or see page 161)
½ teaspoon carom seeds
4 green chiles (see Tip)
4 skinless sea bass fillets, cut in half
2 tomatoes, roughly chopped
1 cup Greek yogurt
cilantro leaves, to garnish
sea salt

YOU'LL ALSO NEED
a piece of charcoal
2 (5-inch) squares of foil

1  Place a skillet over medium heat, add 3 tablespoons of the ghee and cook the onions with a pinch of salt, stirring often, until golden brown—about 10 minutes.

2  Meanwhile, in a bowl, mix together the lemon juice, ginger, garlic, garam masala, carom seeds, and a pinch of salt. Finely chop one of the green chiles and stir it in. Place the fish in a shallow dish and pour over the spicy lemon mixture to coat. Cover and marinate in the refrigerator for 30 minutes.

3  Transfer the cooked onion to a blender, add the tomatoes, yogurt, and remaining green chiles (stems trimmed off first) and blend with a pinch of salt to make a fine paste.

4  Heat 1 tablespoon of the remaining ghee in a sauté pan over medium heat. Stir in the onion paste and 1 cup water and cook for 10 minutes, stirring often, then cover with a lid, reduce the heat and simmer for 5 minutes.

5  Meanwhile, heat your piece of charcoal over a gas flame on the stovetop or in a very hot oven. When hot, place it in a cast-iron or other heatproof dish lined with a double layer of foil. Bring the sides of the foil up to make an open parcel that you can set in the pan with the fish later.

6  Place the fish (discarding the marinade) in the sauté pan and spoon over the warm sauce.

7  Place the charcoal parcel in the center of the pan. Pour ½ teaspoon ghee over it. Cover the pan tightly with a lid and cook the fish over a low heat for 10 minutes.

8  Serve the fish warm with the sauce, garnished with cilantro leaves.

TIP
For a milder heat, discard the chile seeds and membranes.

# FISH POLLICHATHU

SERVES 4

I had a dish like this at one of my favorite restaurants in the south of India. The place is called Jaihind, and you could say it is the Barrafina of India. Mackerel is not a common fish in India, but you do see it on some menus. Since moving to England, both Nirmal and I rate it as one of our favorite fishes, as it takes on spices so well. Try this out—we think you'll agree.

4 whole mackerel, heads removed
1 teaspoon chile powder
½ teaspoon turmeric powder
½ teaspoon ground coriander
½ teaspoon crushed black pepper
3 tablespoons freshly squeezed lemon juice
½ cup coconut or canola oil
1 teaspoon yellow mustard seed
1 onion, finely chopped
1 tablespoon freshly grated ginger
1 green chile, finely chopped
4 garlic cloves, finely minced
1 large tomato, chopped
4 cups sunflower oil, for deep-frying the fish (optional)
1 tablespoon dried curry leaves
sea salt

1 Clean the mackerel and, using a sharp knife, make four diagonal, ½ inch-deep slits on each side of all the fish.

2 In a shallow dish, mix together the chile powder, turmeric, ground coriander, black pepper, lemon juice, and a pinch of salt. Spoon half of this marinade into a bowl and let sit. Add the fish to the original dish and turn to coat thoroughly in the mixture. Cover and marinate in the refrigerator for 30 minutes.

3 Heat the coconut or canola oil in a skillet over medium heat. Add the mustard seeds and wait for them to pop, then add the onion and cook for 5–10 minutes or until soft and a little golden. Stir in the ginger, chile, and garlic and cook for an additional 2–3 minutes, then add the reserved marinade and the tomatoes and cook for 10–15 minutes or until the tomato has cooked down to a thick sauce. Add 1–2 tablespoons water if the sauce gets a little too thick. Take off the heat and cool a little, then blend in a blender or food processor to make a coarse paste.

4 Rub the paste all over the marinated fish and marinate for an additional 30 minutes in the refrigerator.

5 Place the oil for deep-frying in a wide, deep pot and heat until bubbling. Deep-fry the fish, one at a time, for 4–5 minutes, then remove with a slotted spoon and drain on paper towels. Fry the curry leaves in the hot oil until crispy and drain in the same way. Alternatively, roast the fish in an oven preheated to 350°F for 10–12 minutes, turning half way through.

6 Serve hot, scattered with the crispy curry leaves.

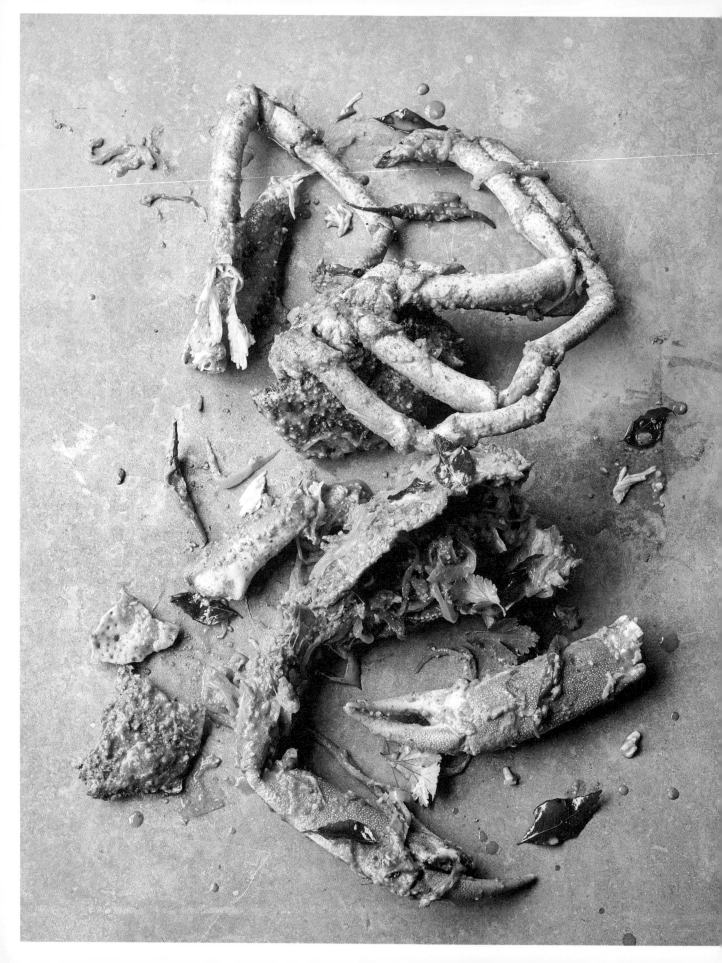

# BLUE CRAB MALABAR CURRY

SERVES 2

The flavors of this dish are quite special, with lots of fresh coconut and a complex spice medley (but don't worry, it's easy to make). I love having this with some sort of dosa (see page 86) or appam to mop up every last drop of sauce.

1¼ cups coconut oil
3 tablespoons freshly grated ginger
5 garlic cloves, finely chopped
5 green chiles, cut in half lengthwise
5 onions, thinly sliced
4 large tomatoes, finely diced
3 tablespoons ground coriander
3 tablespoons chile powder
1 tablespoon Madras curry powder (store-bought, or use our All-in-one Curry Powder, page 157)
1 tablespoon turmeric powder
2 pounds blue or spider crab, cut into 4 pieces
2 cups (5 ounces) grated fresh coconut (see page 51)
1 tablespoon garam masala (store-bought, or see page 161)
1 teaspoon freshly ground black pepper
1 teaspoon ground fennel (see Note)
3 sprigs of fresh curry leaves or 3 tablespoons dried curry leaves
5 tablespoons freshly chopped cilantro
sea salt

1 Place a heavy-bottomed sauté pan over medium heat. Add the coconut oil, ginger, garlic, and green chiles and cook, stirring, for a minute, then fold in the onions and tomatoes and sauté until both have cooked down, about 10 minutes.

2 Stir in the ground coriander, chile powder, Madras curry powder, and turmeric, then add the crab pieces and pour in enough water to just cover. Gently stir and then leave to cook for 20–25 minutes.

3 Meanwhile, in a separate, non-stick skillet, dry-roast the grated coconut over high heat until fragrant and just golden. Let sit to cool, then transfer to a blender, add 2–3 tablespoons water water and blend to a smooth paste.

4 When the crab is cooked, add the roasted coconut paste, garam masala, black pepper, ground fennel, curry leaves, and 3 tablespoons of the chopped cilantro. Stir and simmer for 5 minutes until the sauce thickens.

5 Divide between serving plates and garnish with the remaining cilantro. A few crisp fried curry leaves (see page 110) are also delicious scattered on top.

## NOTE

To make 1 teaspoon ground fennel, grind 2 teaspoons fennel seeds in a spice or coffee grinder or mortar and pestle.

# GRILLED SEABASS IN BANANA LEAF

SERVES 2

This is a wonderful, light dish and great on the barbecue—especially for pescatarians. The banana leaf pocket keeps the fish wonderfully tender. Of course, you can also cook this in a skillet, as noted below, or even roast it in the oven. No banana leaf? Just use foil or parchment paper, or any other edible leaf like large fig or vine (grape) leaves. *Pictured on pages 118–119.*

2 whole sea bass (approx. ½ pound), cleaned
3½ ounces fresh cilantro, roughly chopped
¼ cup fresh mint leaves
4 garlic cloves, peeled
1 tablespoon freshly grated ginger
1–2 green chiles, finely chopped
½ teaspoon crushed black pepper
1 teaspoon cumin seeds
¼ teaspoon turmeric powder
3 tablespoons freshly squeezed lemon juice
2 tablespoons ghee, melted
2 tablespoons Greek yogurt
2 (11-inch square) banana leaf
your choice of raita, to serve
   (see pages 176–183)
sea salt

1 Take each sea bass in turn and, using a sharp knife, score the fish four times with ½ inch-deep slashes across both sides.

2 Place the cilantro, mint, garlic, ginger, chile, black pepper, cumin seeds, turmeric, lemon juice, and a pinch of salt in a blender or food processor and blend into a fine paste. Stir through the melted ghee and yogurt and check the seasoning.

3 Gently warm the banana leaves over a gas flame on the stovetop for 10–20 seconds on each side, ensuring that they don't burn.

4 Place each sea bass in the center of a banana leaf and divide the cilantro mixture between the two. Slather it all over, inside and out, then wrap the banana leaf around the fish like a pocket (you can tie it together with string). Leave to marinate for 30 minutes.

5 Preheat your oven broiler to high, set a grill pan over high heat, or use a barbecue. When hot, broil the sea bass pockets for 7–8 minutes on both sides. Serve warm with raita on the side.

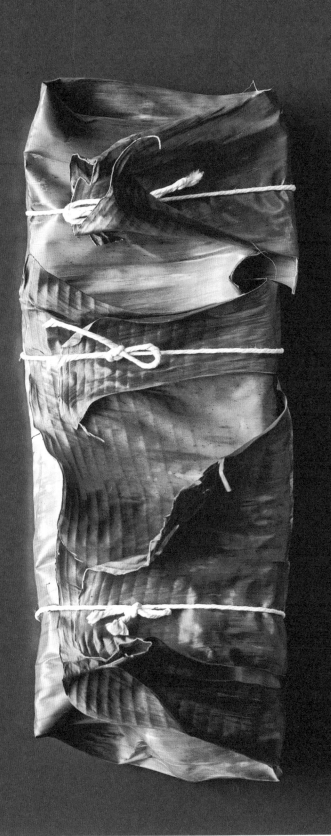

# COCONUT SAMBAL-STUFFED POMFRET

This recipe is from southern India, where coconut features in so many dishes. Pomfret is a celebrated fish on our shores, as it comes from the Indian Ocean. You can also use sea bass, which is similar and works beautifully.

2 pomfret or sea bass, cleaned
canola or sunflower oil, for frying
seasonal greens, to serve

FOR THE MARINADE
2 tablespoons canola or olive oil
1 green chile
1 teaspoon tamarind paste
2 garlic cloves, finely minced
2 teaspoons freshly grated ginger
a pinch of sea salt

FOR THE COCONUT CHUTNEY
½ cup grated fresh coconut (see page 51)
   or dried coconut
1 ounce freshly chopped cilantro leaves
1 green chile, finely chopped
1 garlic clove, finely minced
½ teaspoon cumin seeds
1 tablespoon freshly diced mango
½ teaspoon superfine sugar
a pinch of sea salt

FOR THE COATING
⅓ cup all-purpose flour
⅓ cup semolina
½ teaspoon turmeric powder
a pinch of chile powder
½ teaspoon sea salt

1 Take each fish in turn and, using a sharp knife, make a deep cut to create a pocket either side of the central bone. Make four additional light cuts on both sides to help the fish cook evenly and to absorb all the flavors of the marinade.

2 Place all the marinade ingredients in a mortar and pestle and grind together to make a fine paste. Slather all over the fish until thoroughly coated. Leave to marinate for 30 minutes.

3 Wipe the mortar and pestle clean and add all the chutney ingredients, then mash with as little water as possible to make a smooth paste. Stuff the mixture into the pockets you've made in each fish.

4 Mix together all the coating ingredients on a large, flat plate, then dredge each fish in the seasoned flour and let sit.

5 Place a large skillet over medium heat and add enough oil to fully coat the pan. Fry one fish at a time, cooking for 4 minutes on each side or until it is cooked through—pierce the thickest piece to see if the flesh is white, a little firm and flakes from the bone. Serve straight away with a plate of seasonal greens.

# MALABAR SHRIMP PULAO

SERVES 4

Nirmal and I ate this when we were travelling around the Maharashtra in Western India. Normally I prefer meat in a pulao, one that slowly cooks and renders down until it just falls apart, but this one kicks ass. The magic is in the shrimp stock, which is made with the heads and shells—this is where the flavor lies.

FOR THE MARINATED SHRIMP
12 raw jumbo shrimp in
    their shells
5 garlic cloves, finely minced
1 teaspoon finely grated ginger
½ teaspoon turmeric powder
¾ teaspoon chile powder
1 tablespoon olive or canola oil
sea salt

FOR THE SHRIMP STOCK
2 teaspoons turmeric powder
½ teaspoon chile powder

FOR THE PULAO
½ cup olive or canola oil
6 whole green cardamom pods
1 cinnamon stick
8 cloves
2 onions, finely chopped
2 green chiles, finely chopped
5 garlic cloves, finely minced
1 tablespoon freshly grated ginger
1 teaspoon turmeric powder
1 tablespoon ground coriander
4 tomatoes, finely diced
2½ ounces grated fresh coconut (see
    page 51), plus extra to garnish
½ pound brown basmati rice, washed
    and soaked for half an hour
1 tablespoon freshly squeezed lime
    juice
15 mint leaves
sea salt, to taste
6 tablespoons chopped cilantro, to
    garnish
your choice of raita, to serve
    (see pages 176–183)

1  Remove the heads and shells from the shrimp and set them aside to use in the stock.

2  In a bowl, mix together the garlic, ginger, turmeric, chile powder, oil, and a pinch of salt. Fold in the shelled shrimp and marinate for 30 minutes.

3  For the stock, pour 6½ cups water into a large pot and add the shrimp heads and shells along with the turmeric, chile powder, and a pinch of salt. Bring to the boil, then simmer for 15–20 minutes. Strain the stock and let sit.

4  For the rice, place a large flameproof casserole pot or pan with a lid over high heat. Add the oil, reduce the heat and cook the cardamom, cinnamon, and cloves for a minute until fragrant. Stir in the onions and gently fry for 5 minutes until lightly caramelized. Add the green chiles and cook for a minute, then add the garlic and ginger and cook, stirring, for an additional minute. Fold in the turmeric and ground coriander.

5  Add the tomatoes and 1 tablespoon water to deglaze the pan. Cook for 5 minutes until the tomatoes have broken down, then stir in the grated coconut and cook for a minute.

6  Drain the rice and add to the pot. Turn up the heat, add the shrimp stock and stir well, then cover with a lid and cook for 25 minutes until the rice is tender and the pulao looks like a loose risotto—you can add a little extra water, if necessary.

7  Stir the marinated shrimps into the pulao, adding all the marinating spices, too. Fold in the lime juice and mint leaves and cook over low heat for 5–7 minutes or until the shrimps are cooked through. Season with salt and serve warm, scattered with the chopped cilantro and with a bowl of raita on the side.

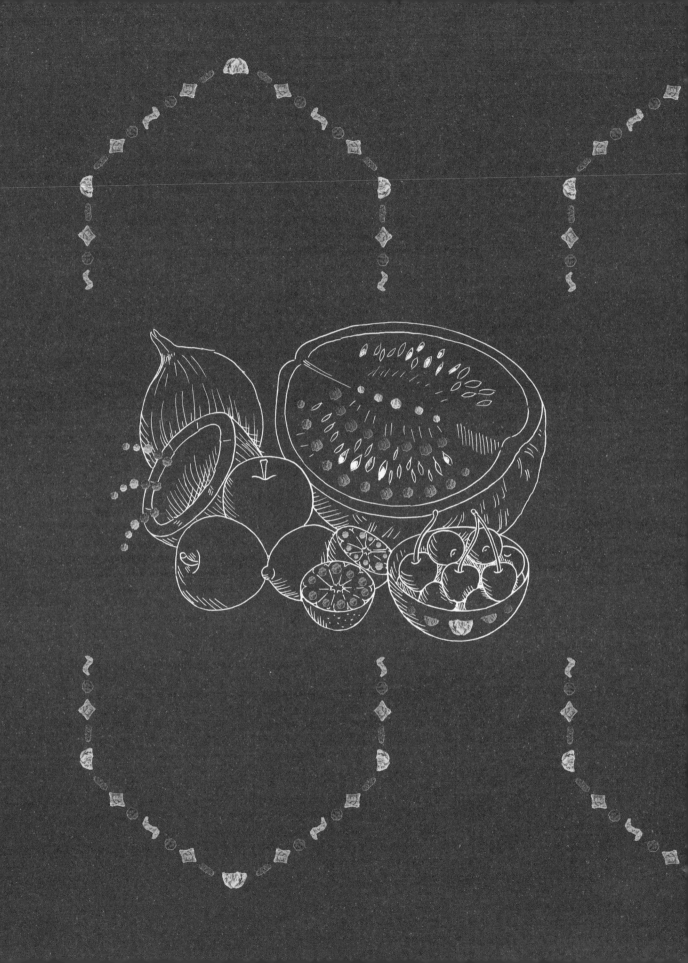

# SWEET PLATES
# AND DRINKS

# SWEET PLATES
# AND DRINKS

In India, we love sweet things. Meals often begin with a cocktail and end with a dessert. This is certainly a tradition we like to uphold in the restaurant. The drink recipes that follow constitute a tapestry woven with ideas based on classic recipes combined with some inspired by stories of people and places, traditions and tales.

The desserts veer further away from the familiar, though all have Indian roots. You will find some of the key flavors and ingredients from the savory chapters making a welcome return in this sweet one.

These drinks and sweet plates provide the perfect bookends for the main dishes sandwiched in this tome.

# MASALA CHAAS

SERVES 2

In the north of India we have lassi, but in the south it's all about chaas, which is really refreshing. While similar to lassi, chaas is a bit lighter and can be either sweet or savory. This one's in the latter category, and is a healthy blend of spices, herbs, and yogurt. It's sure to cool you on a hot day. *Pictured on page 129 (right).*

1¼ cup Greek or plain yogurt
¼ teaspoon black or a good-quality sea salt
1 teaspoon chaat masala
1 teaspoon freshly grated ginger
1 green chile, finely chopped
a pinch of asafoetida
1 teaspoon freshly squeezed lime juice

TO GARNISH
2 sprigs of curry leaves (fresh are best if you can get them, but dried are fine)
2 tablespoons freshly chopped cilantro

1 Place all the ingredients except the curry leaves and cilantro in a blender and blend until smooth. Add ½ cup water to thin the mixture a little and blitz again. Chill until ready to serve.

2 To serve, divide the mixture between two glasses and garnish each with a sprig of curry leaves and some cilantro leaves.

# AAM PANNA

## with SAFFRON AND CARDAMOM

SERVES 4

Mango lassis are typically made with a sweet mango purée like this one, but the aam panna here is elevated by a beautiful blend of spices. We also serve it mixed with water instead of yogurt. If you like, it can be turned into a wonderful cocktail. I love it with vodka.

1 ripe mango, peeled and pit removed
¼ cup sugar
ground seeds from 6 cardamom pods
4 saffron strands
a large pinch of freshly ground black pepper
a pinch of sea salt or black salt

1  Place the mango flesh in a blender with the sugar, cardamom, saffron, black pepper, and salt and blend until smooth.

2  To serve, spoon 2–3 tablespoons of the spiced mango purée into each glass and stir in ⅔ cup water. Adjust the concentration of the mango purée to suit your taste. Serve cold over ice.

3  You can store any remaining mango purée in an airtight container in the refrigerator for up to 1 week.

# MINT AND APPLE LASSI

SERVES 4

We've taken a classic lassi and given it an English twist. This one is really refreshing. If you want to give it a quirky boost, swap the apple syrup for a splash of cider instead.

4 green apples, peeled, cored and chopped, plus extra to garnish
2⅔ cups Greek yogurt
2 teaspoons superfine sugar
2 tablespoons Monin apple syrup (see Tip)
¼ cup fresh mint leaves, plus extra to garnish
2 handfuls of ice cubes

1 Place the apple, yogurt, sugar, apple syrup, mint, and ice in a high-speed blender and blitz until smooth.

2 Spoon a little chopped apple in the bottom of four glasses and pour the lassi on top. Serve right away, garnished with a mint sprig.

NOTE

If you can't find Monin apple syrup, you can substitute it for apple juice and add a tablespoon more of superfine sugar to the mixture.

# COCONUT KHUS

Khus syrup is a dark green syrup with a sweet, woody flavor and scent. It is made from an extract of the roots of vetiver grass, which is closely related to sorghum but shares many characteristics with other fragrant grasses, such as lemongrass and citronella. It's really refreshing here married with coconut and vanilla ice cream. You can find khus syrup in Indian syrups or online—it's worth seeking out for its unique flavor.

2 cups coconut water
2¼ cups coconut cream
1 tablespoon freshly squeezed lime juice
4 teaspoons khus syrup (see intro)
4 scoops of vanilla ice cream
4 red cherries
2 tablespoons grated fresh coconut (see page 51) or dried coconut

1 Place the coconut water, coconut cream, and lime juice in a blender and blitz together until smooth.

2 Take four tall glasses and place 1 teaspoon of khus syrup in the bottom of each. Divide the coconut mixture between the four glasses and finish with a scoop of vanilla ice cream, a red cherry and a sprinkling of grated coconut. Serve immediately.

# KASHMIRI KAHWA

My mum loves this drink. She lives in northern Indian, where it's much cooler, and this is what she drinks to warm her up. We call it "cola" as it's made with brown sugar and all the spices—it's like a healthier take on the classic soda. If you prefer, you can cut the sugar in this right down or swap it out for honey.

½ cinnamon stick
2 green cardamom pods, bruised
2 cloves
2 tablespoons brown sugar
4 teaspoons green tea leaves or
    2 good-quality green tea bags
a large pinch of saffron, soaked in
    1 tablespoon warm water for
    10 minutes
3 tablespoons flaked almonds
a few fresh mint leaves, to garnish

1  Pour 2¼ cups water into a pot and place over medium heat. Add the cinnamon, cardamom, cloves and sugar. Bring to the boil, then reduce the heat and simmer for 5 minutes.

2  Add the green tea leaves or tea bags, mix well and simmer for 4 minutes, stirring occasionally. Strain the tea, add the saffron (along with its soaking liquid) and almond flakes and serve warm, garnished with a few mint leaves.

# WATERMELON SHIKANJI

This is what Indian mothers give their children instead of cola. It's a really cooling drink for when you've come home after being out in the heat.

1 (2 pound) watermelon, peeled and cubed
8 teaspoons freshly squeezed lime juice
5 teaspoons honey
a pinch of black salt (optional)
1 teaspoon roasted cumin seeds, crushed
2¼ cups soda or sparkling water
ice cubes, to serve
mint leaves, to garnish

1 Place the watermelon in a food processor or blender and blitz to a purée. Strain into a jug and then whisk in the lime juice, honey, salt, and crushed cumin seeds.

2 Stir in the soda or sparkling water. Pour into four tall glasses over ice and garnish with fresh mint.

# KITTY PARTY BELLINI

SERVES 6

In India, there's a tradition between ladies who lunch. Once a month, they each take turn hosting a party at home, known as a "Kitty" party. The "kitty" refers to a collection of money made by the guests and paid to the host to cover the costs of holding the party. Typically, these parties start with a glass of fizz, which is the inspiration for this beautiful bellini.

¾ cup mango crush (see Note)
2 tablespoon freshly chopped cilantro
2 slices of fresh green chile, plus extra to garnish
1 (750 ml) bottle of prosecco

1 Place the mango crush, cilantro, and chile in a blender and blend until smooth. Divide between six champagne glasses, allowing 2 tablespoons per glass.

2 Top up with chilled prosecco. Garnish each glass with a slice of green chile.

# PANI PURI MARGARITA

SERVES 1

Holi is a Hindu festival celebrated in the spring, also known as the "festival of colors" or the "festival of love". It signifies the victory of good over evil and the arrival of spring and end of winter. For many it's a festive day to meet others, play and laugh, forget and forgive, and repair broken relationships. During the festival people throw brightly colored paint powders at each other, as well as water (to help the paint stick). Quite often, you'll find people lacing the water with alcohol, which has inspired this wonderful cocktail. We garnish it with crushed pani puri, a crispy Indian street food snack that is often served at Holi festivals. It makes a delicious finish.

2 tablespoons tequila
2 tablespoons Cointreau
2 tablespoons tamarind paste
1 tablespoon freshly squeezed lime juice

TO GARNISH
a pinch of Gunpowder Spice Mix (see page 158)
a thin slice of lime, twisted
a pinch of crushed puri (optional; available in Indian supermarkets and online)

1 Place all the ingredients except the garnishes into a cocktail shaker with some ice. Vigorously shake for 10 seconds.

2 Pour into a tumbler packed full of ice. Garnish with the Gunpowder spice, twist of lime and a dusting of crushed puri, if using.

## NOTE

You can find mango crush or similar mango cocktail pre-mixed blends in most grocey stores and liquor stores. Or you can make your own by puréeing the flesh from a ripe mango with 5 tablespoons water and 5 tablespoons sugar, or more or less, to taste. Store in a sealed clean bottle in the refrigerator for up to 3 days, or freeze until ready to use.

# BOW BARRACKS GIMLET

# GUNPOWDER REGIMENT

SERVES 1

SERVES 1

The Bow Barracks was a garrison's mess built for the army during World War I, located in Kolkata. If you wanted a gimlet, which is what this cocktail is based on, you'd go to the Bow Barracks.

Rum and coke was an army staple and the rum of choice used to be Hercules, which was distilled exclusively for the army. Old Monk was launched in the 1950s and has been an iconic drink in India ever since. It is worth seeking out a bottle if you can, but you can use another dark rum here if needed.

3 tablespoons Bombay Sapphire
1 teaspoon freshly squeezed lime juice
2 tablespoons ginger syrup (see Note)
A few thin lime slices, to garnish

2 tablespoons Old Monk rum, or other dark rum
3 pinches Gunpowder Spice Mix (see page 158)
1 tablespoon freshly squeezed lime juice
1 cup Coca-Cola

1  Pour all the ingredients except the lime into a cocktail shaker with some ice. Shake for 10 seconds. Pour into cold tumblers packed with ice.

TO GARNISH
a thin slice of lemon, twisted
a pinch of chile powder

2  Garnish with the twist of lime.

1  Fill a tumbler with ice. Pour in the rum, spice mix and lime. Top up with cola.

2  Garnish with the twist of lemon and a pinch of chile powder.

NOTE
You can use the syrup from a jar of stem ginger or make up a homemade syrup by simmering ½ cup superfine sugar with ½ cup water and 4 tablespoons grated fresh ginger for 10 minutes. While still warm, strain the syrup through a strainer into a sterilized jar, filling it to the top, then seal. It will keep for 3 months in a cool place.

# MASALA CHAI AND GINGER PORRIDGE

SERVES 2–4

We love our tea in India, especially chai, but children aren't allowed to drink tea. This was my mother's way of letting us have a little taste of it. We serve this for breakfast, but it's so delicious that it could easily double up as a dessert.

1 cup (7 ounces) bulgur wheat
4 cups almond milk
2 tablespoons ghee
2 tablespoons candied ginger,
    finely chopped
4 masala chai tea bags
a pinch of sea salt

TO SERVE
crushed pistachio nuts
toasted flaked almonds
fresh berries

1  Place a large pot with a lid over medium heat. Add the bulgur wheat, almond milk, ghee, candied ginger, tea bags, and a pinch of salt and bring to a gentle simmer. Reduce the heat, cover and cook for about 20 minutes, stirring occasionally, until the grains are tender and creamy. Top up with additional milk or water during cooking, if needed.

2  Lift out the tea bags and use a fork to squeeze them against the side of the pot to release all their flavor. Stir the porridge.

3  Divide the porridge between two to four bowls and serve topped with crushed pistachios, toasted flaked almonds, and fresh berries.

# BAKED PANEER CHEESECAKE

SERVES 12

This is my mom's recipe. My parents traveled quite a lot and my mum would always pick up inspiration from her trips. Of course, she's given it an Indian twist by using paneer in the cheesecake and lots of cardamom. It's a stunning dessert.

10½ ounces graham crackers
ground seeds from 4 green
  cardamom pods
2 drops of vanilla extract
½ cup unsalted butter, melted

FOR THE CHEESECAKE TOPPING
14 ounces full-fat cream cheese
6 ounces sour cream
7 ounces paneer, finely grated
¾ cup superfine sugar
ground seeds from 8 cardamom
  pods
1 tablespoon vanilla extract
3 eggs

TO SERVE
crushed pistachio nuts
cherry or mango fruit compote
  (optional)

1 Line a 9-inch springform tin with parchment paper, allowing enough excess to overhang the edges of the tin to make it easy to remove.

2 Place the biscuits, cardamom, and vanilla in a food processor and blitz until finely crushed. Add the melted butter and process until well combined and the crumbs stick together when pressed.

3 Transfer the graham cracker mixture to the lined tin, using the back of a spoon to spread and press it firmly over the base and up the sides of the tin. Cover with plastic wrap and place in the refrigerator for 30 minutes to chill.

4 Meanwhile, preheat the oven to 300°F.

5 Place the cream cheese, sour cream, grated paneer, sugar, cardamom, and vanilla in the cleaned bowl of the food processor and process until smooth. Whisk in the eggs, adding them one by one, until well combined.

6 Pour the cream cheese mixture into the chilled biscuit base and spread it evenly. Bake for 1 hour or until it has set completely.

7 Turn off the oven and leave the cheesecake inside until it has cooled completely before removing.

8 Chill for 4–5 hours in the refrigerator before removing from the tin and serving. The cheesecake is delicious topped with a scattering of crushed pistachios or with a fruit compote, like mango or cherry,

# MASALA CHAI CRÈME BRÛLÉE

MAKES 4–6

I'm a big custard fan. Anything with custard wins me over. This is just wonderful—chai goes so well in desserts. You could also add white chocolate to the mix in place of some of the sugar.

3 cloves
5 cardamom pods
1 cinnamon stick or 1 teaspoon
  ground cinnamon
1¾ cups heavy cream
½ cup whole milk
2 Indian masala chai teabags
½ teaspoon ground ginger
½ cup superfine sugar, plus 5
  tablespoons for the tops
5 large egg yolks
½ teaspoon vanilla extract
biscuits, cookies or shortbread, to
  serve (optional)

1 Preheat the oven to 300°F.

2 Place the cloves, cardamom, and cinnamon in a spice or coffee grinder or mortar and pestle and grind to a fine powder.

3 Pour the cream and milk into a large pot. Add the tea bags, ground whole spices, and ginger and stir to mix well. Place the pot over medium heat and bring almost to the boil, then reduce the heat and simmer for 5 minutes. Let sit to infuse further for 10 minutes, then strain the mixture through a strainer or muslin cloth.

4 In a large bowl, whisk the sugar, egg yolks, and vanilla until light and creamy. Slowly pour the strained cream into the egg mixture, whisking continuously, then divide the mixture between 4–6 small ramekins.

5 Place the ramekins in a roasting dish and pour enough boiling water into the tray to reach halfway up the sides of the ramekins. Place the tray on the middle shelf of the oven and bake for 30 minutes until just set, but with a slight wobble.

6 Let sit to cool to room temperature before chileng in the refrigerator for a final set.

7 To finish, sprinkle enough sugar on the top of each crème brûlée to fully cover the surface of the set cream. Caramelize with either a kitchen blowtorch or under a very hot oven broiler. Serve straight away or return to the refrigerator until ready to eat. Serve with your choice of biscuits, cookies or shortbread, if you like.

# SPICED RHUBARB

## with CREAMY SAGO CUSTARD

SERVES 4

Nirmal devised this recipe for me, as he knows how much I love custard. The rhubarb here is very much inspired by the British seasons. You get versions of rhubarb in the north of India, but it's not common.

FOR THE CUSTARD
¾ cup plus 2 tablespoons whole milk
7 ounces small tapioca pearls,
    soaked overnight and drained
1 cup plus 2 tablespoons heavy
    cream
2 medium eggs, well beaten,
    plus 1 medium egg yolk
½ cup white jaggery or sugar
1 vanilla pod

FOR THE SPICED RHUBARB
1¼ cups red wine
½ cup light brown sugar
grated zest of 1 orange
1 cinnamon stick
1 star anise
1 bay leaf
3 cloves
10 rhubarb stalks, trimmed and
    cut into 1-inch pieces
a pinch of sea salt
2 tablespoons crushed
    pistachios, to serve

1  First make the custard. Pour the milk into a saucepan set over medium heat. Once it's warm but not boiling, add the tapioca pearls and simmer gently for 10 minutes or until the pearls are tender. Stir in the cream over low heat.

2  In a bowl, whisk the whole eggs and extra egg yolk with the jaggery, then fold the mixture into the creamy tapioca. Add the vanilla pod and gently boil for 3 minutes, stirring continuously, then take off the heat. Pour into a bowl and cover the surface with plastic wrap to prevent a skin forming, then leave to cool. Chill in the refrigerator until set.

3  For the spiced rhubarb, place the wine, brown sugar, orange zest, and whole spices in a large saucepan, bring to the boil, and stir until the sugar has dissolved.

4  Add the rhubarb and salt, then reduce the heat and simmer for about 9 minutes until the rhubarb is tender. With a slotted spoon, transfer the rhubarb to a shallow dish, arranging it in a single layer.

5  Boil the wine syrup in the saucepan for about 5 minutes until it reduces and thickens. Pour the syrup over the rhubarb and let sit to cool, then cover and chill in the refrigerator until cold.

6  Place a spoonful of compote in the bottom of four tall glasses or jars. Top with a spoonful of tapioca custard and repeat these layers until you reach the top. Finish with a scattering of crushed pistachios and serve right away.

# DARK CHOCOLATE AND CINNAMON BAR
## with PASSION FRUIT SHRIKHAND SAGO

SERVES 6

Chocolate doesn't feature so much in traditional Indian desserts, but we couldn't resist orchestrating a few chocolate masterpieces for the Gunpowder menu. The chocolate bar here is like a slice of heaven— a melt-in-your mouth truffle-turned-cake that's scented with cinnamon and will make your taste buds sing. Paired with the sharp passion fruit shrikhand, which is a traditional Indian strained yogurt from Maharashtra and Gujarat, typically served at weddings, Nirmal has created a symphony of texture and flavor.

FOR THE PASSION FRUIT SHRIKHAND
2 cups Greek yogurt
2-3 fresh passion fruits
½ cup powdered sugar
¼ teaspoon ground cardamom
   seeds

FOR THE DARK CHOCOLATE
AND CINNAMON BAR
13 ounces dark chocolate
⅔ cup whole milk
2 cups heavy cream
¼ cup superfine sugar
1 teaspoon vanilla extract
½ teaspoon ground cinnamon
2 whole eggs

TO SERVE
6 tablespoons crushed honeycomb
   (optional)

1 Pour the yogurt into a muslin cloth. Gather up the sides of the muslin and tie together with a string at the top. Hang over a bowl in the refrigerator for 12 hours or overnight so that all the whey drains off the yogurt, giving you a thick labneh to use as the base for the shrikhand.

2 Halve the passion fruit. Scoop out the seedy pulp from the center and press it through a strainer to remove the seeds and give you a fresh passion fruit purée. You will need 4 tablespoons of this.

3 Once the labneh has finished straining, transfer it to a bowl (discarding the whey) and mix it with the passion fruit puree. Sift in the icing sugar and cardamom. Cover and chill until ready to serve.

4 Break the chocolate into small pieces and add to a heatproof bowl. Set the bowl over a pot containing a shallow pool of gently simmering water, over low heat. Stir the chocolate often until fully melted. Let sit.

5 Pour the milk and cream into a separate pot with the sugar, vanilla, and cinnamon. Simmer gently over medium heat until the mixture just starts to bubble.

6 Whisk the whole eggs and egg yolk together in a large bowl. As the milk and cream mixture comes to the boil, pour it over the eggs, then whisk the mixture until smooth and thick. Fold the melted chocolate through.

7 Pour the chocolate mixture into a 9 inch-square dish lined with parchment paper. Gently tap the dish on the work surface to release the air bubbles, then chill in the refrigerator for 6–12 hours or, for best results, overnight.

8 To serve, remove the chocolate bar from the refrigerator and cut into squares or rectangles. Serve with a heaped spoonful of the passion fruit shrikhand.

9 For an added presentational flourish, serve dusted with crushed honeycomb.

# BANANA AND CURRY LEAF PARFAIT
## with CHOCOLATE MOUSSE

SERVES 6

This is one of Nirmal's works of art and it's the perfect dessert to make if you're wanting to woo someone. It's a dance of three amazing flavors: bananas, chocolate, and pistachio, intermingled with the fragrance of curry leaves, which work here just as a thyme or rosemary wand is waved upon a sweet pudding to cast an earthy, aromatic spell.

FOR THE BANANA AND
CURRY LEAF PARFAIT
2 ounces peeled, ripe banana
1 tablespoon freshly squeezed lime
   juice
5 ounces heavy cream
1 egg white
⅓ cup superfine sugar
6 fried curry leaves
1 pinch curry powder (see page 157)

FOR THE DARK CHOCOLATE MOUSSE
8 ounces dark chocolate
3 tablespoons cocoa powder
1½ cups thick heavy cream
2 tablespoons golden syrup
1 cup unsalted butter, slightly
   softened
¼ teaspoon ground cardamom
   seeds

FOR THE PISTACHIO CHIKKI
9 ounces shelled pistachios
scant 1 cup superfine sugar
1 tablespoon ghee
A pinch of saffron strands
Ground seeds of 2 cardamom pods

1  In a bowl, mash or purée the banana with half the lime juice until you have a rough purée. Whip the cream until it holds its shape but is still a little soft.

2  In another, very clean bowl and using a very clean electric whisk, beat the egg white with the remaining lime juice until stiff. Slowly add the sugar until you have a stiff and shiny meringue texture.

3  Gently fold the whipped cream and egg white mixture together, then add the banana, curry leaves, and curry powder and mix well.

4  Divide the mixture between six small ramekins lined with parchment paper. Pop into the freezer to set overnight.

5  For the mousse, finely chop the chocolate and place in a heatproof bowl with the cocoa powder. Pour the cream and syrup into a small pot and gently heat until it just starts to bubble. Remove from the heat and immediately pour the hot cream mixture over the chocolate. Leave to stand until the chocolate is melted, about 2–3 minutes.

6  Whisk the chocolate and cream mixture by hand until completely smooth, then let sit to cool to room temperature. Once cooled, add the softened butter and ground

cardamom to the chocolate mixture and beat using a handmixer, or vigorously by hand, until the mousse is completely smooth and silky.

7  Pop the mousse into the freezer for 5 minutes, then stir with a rubber spatula. Repeat three or four more times to reach the desired mousse consistency. Once nicely chilled, give the mousse a final whip until it is light and fluffy.

8  For the chikki, roughly chop the pistachios. Set a skillet over medium heat. Add half the ghee and, once melted, stir in the pistachios. Gently fry until lightly colored, then spoon onto a plate to cool.

9  Return the pan to the heat and add the remaining ghee. Add the sugar and 2 teaspoons water. Stir briskly until all the sugar melts and turns a golden brown. Fold the saffron and ground cardamom into the sugar, along with the nuts.

10  Pour the mixture onto a baking sheet lined with parchment paper. Let sit to harden. Break into pieces with a kitchen hammer.

11  To serve, remove the banana parfait from the freezer and ease from their moulds onto plates. Serve a dollop of mousse next to each parfait and decorate with a dusting of the pistachio chikki.

# CHERRY AND ALMOND GHEE CAKE

Ghee is a superfood. It builds the bones and can heal the gut. We've used it in this cake in place of butter, which gives the cake an extra-rich taste. We've added a little bit of all-purpose flour to the cake to lighten it, but if you can't eat wheat or gluten, you can swap it out for more ground almonds.

2 large eggs
½ cup superfine sugar
zest from 2 lemons
ground seeds from 8 green cardamom pods
½ cup ghee, melted
½ cup all-purpose flour
1¼ cup ground almonds
35 pitted cherries, plus more to serve
vanilla ice cream, to serve

1 Preheat the oven to 350°F and line a 10-inch square tray or 6-inch round cake pan with parchment paper.

2 In a large metal or glass bowl, whisk together the eggs, sugar, lemon zest, and cardamom until light and fluffy.

3 Slowly whisk in the melted ghee and then fold in the flour and ground almonds until just combined.

4 Pour the cake mixture into the prepared pan and spread it out evenly. Dot with pitted cherries all over the surface.

5 Bake the cake in the center of the oven for 35 minutes until golden and baked through. To test it is baked through, insert a skewer into the middle—it should come out clean

6 Serve warm with vanilla ice cream and cherry compote or more fresh cherries.

# MANGO MURABBA BAKED CHEESE CAKE

SERVES 12

Cheesecake is a family favorite—we make this all the time, and as the seasons roll by, we swap out the mango pulp and chutney for other fruity flavors like pineapple or even apples or pears. Dates also work a treat here. You can use this as a base for all sorts of incarnations.

10 ounces graham crackers
2 drops of vanilla extract or the seeds from 1 pod
7 tablespoons unsalted butter, melted
17 ounces full-fat cream cheese
10½ ounces sour cream
scant 1 cup superfine sugar
3½ ounces mango chutney
4 medium eggs
3 tablespoons mango pulp (see Note)

1 Line a 9-inch springform tin with parchment paper, allowing enough excess to overhang the edges of the tin to make it easy to remove.

2 Place the graham crackers and vanilla in a food processor and blitz until finely crushed. Add the melted butter and process until well combined and the crumbs stick together when pressed.

3 Transfer the mixture to the lined tin, using the back of a spoon to spread and press it firmly over the base and up the sides of the tin. Cover with plastic wrap and place in the refrigerator for 30 minutes to chill.

4 Meanwhile, preheat the oven to 300°F.

5 Place the cream cheese, sour cream, sugar, and mango chutney in the cleaned bowl of the food processor and process until smooth. Whisk in the eggs, adding them one by one, until well combined.

6 Transfer 4 tablespoons of this cream cheese mixture to a separate bowl. Add the mango pulp and whisk together until well combined. Pour into the case and spread it evenly.

7 Dollop the reserved mango and cream cheese mixture on top, using the tip of a butter knife to ripple it through and create a marble effect.

8 Bake for 1 hour or until it has set completely.

9 Turn off the oven and leave the cheesecake inside until it has cooled completely before removing. Chill for 4–5 hours in the refrigerator before serving.

NOTE

If you can't find store-bought mango pulp make your own by simply pureeing the flesh of a ripe mango with a little sugar, if needed, to sweeten.

# OLD MONK AND MANUKA
# BREAD AND BUTTER PUDDING

SERVES 6

Old Monk Rum is an iconic Indian run, launched in the 1950s. It's a full-flavored dark rum that's aged for a minimum of seven years. It has a distinct vanilla flavor, which makes it a brilliant addition to puddings, especially this comforting bread and butter pudding, which is a marriage of two of my favorite things: custard and rum! My brother is also a sucker for this one. When he comes over from India, he'll dine in the restaurant, order this and ask for an extra portion, which he'll take back with him to devour on the airplane home. The manuka here, by the way, refers to a special variety of raisin found in India. If you can't find manuka raisins, just swap for what you can source.

FOR THE BREAD PUDDING
1¼ cup Old Monk rum (or other dark
    rum), plus 2 tablespoons
¾ cup raisins (use manuka raisins
    if you can find them)
1 tablespoon butter
1½ cups heavy cream
2 cups whole milk
3 medium eggs, plus 3 egg yolks
seeds from 1 vanilla bean or
    1 teaspoon vanilla extract
scant 1 cup superfine sugar
12 ounce brioche loaf, sliced

FOR THE CINNAMON AND RUM SYRUP
1 cup superfine sugar
1 cinnamon stick
a pinch of sea salt

1 Soak the raisins in the 1¼ cup rum overnight. Drain and reserve both the raisins and the rum. (If you don't have time to soak them overnight, place the raisins and rum in a saucepan and simmer over a low heat for 25 minutes.)

2 Grease a 9-inch square baking dish with the butter. In a deep pot, bring the cream, milk, and vanilla to simmering point.

3 In a large bowl, whisk the whole eggs and the egg yolks with the sugar and 2 tablespoons rum. Pour the simmering cream over the egg mixture and whisk until well combined to make a smooth custard.

4 Pour one third of the custard into the prepared pan. Arrange a layer of the brioche slices on top. Sprinkle half the soaked raisins over. Add another layer of custard and brioche. Pour the last third of the custard on top and sprinkle over the remaining raisins.

5 Pop the mixture in the refrigerator for 1 hour so that the bread can soak up all the custard.

6 Meanwhile, gently warm the reserved raisin-soaking rum in a pot with the sugar, cinnamon, ⅓ cup water and a pinch of salt. Bring to the boil and boil for 2 minutes. Take off the heat.

7 Preheat the oven to 350°F. Drizzle 4 tablespoons of the cinnamon and rum syrup over the top of the bread and butter pudding. Slide the pudding into the oven and bake for 45 minutes or until the custard has set and the top is golden brown.

8 Slice and serve with vanilla ice cream, drizzled with some of the remaining cinnamon and rum syrup.

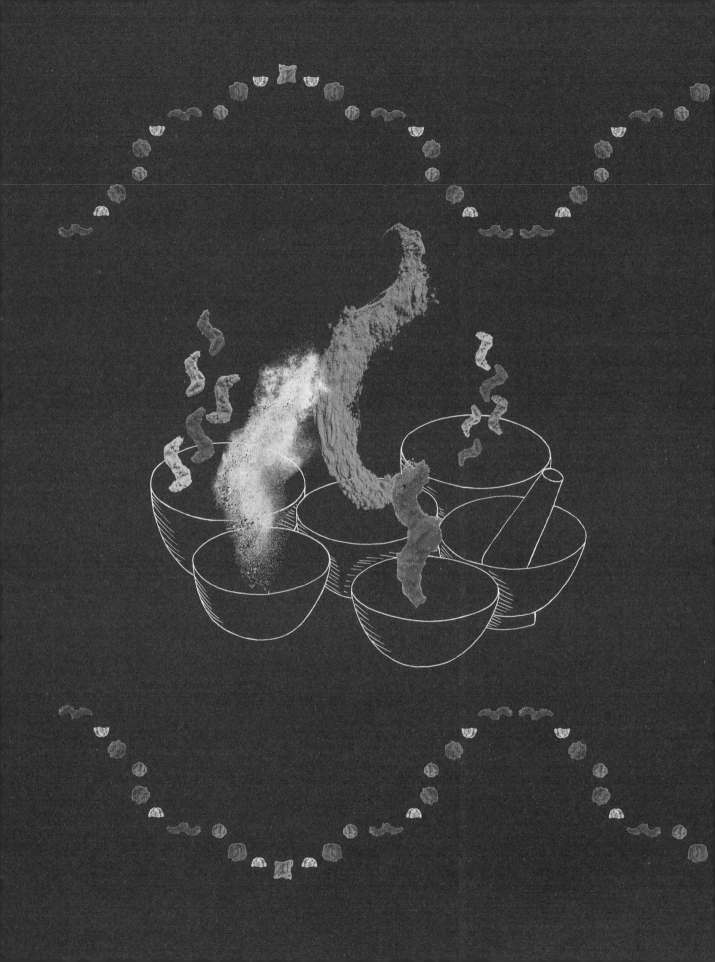

# SIDES AND SPICE

# SIDES
# AND SPICE

There is not a single Indian dish where spices aren't the key ingredients, and while the term "side" sounds like an afterthought, these chutneys, pickles, and raitas that we've curated on the pages that follow are pretty much the pillars of our cuisine.

The recipes we've gathered together for this chapter are rich with family history, as well as flavor. Our grannies, mothers, fathers, and brothers have poured their knowledge and time into perfecting the spice blends that make our food at Gunpowder so unique. Nirmal's family pickle business, and generations of home picklers in both our families, have helped mature our selection of preserves. These, and the raitas we've chosen, are ones we wouldn't dream of not having in our own home refrigerators.

Even if you just have one or two of these spice mixes and side dishes to hand in your kitchen, you'll be able to spin a simple dish into something sublime with a magical sprinkle, spoon, dab, and dollop of these flavor-packed medleys.

# ALL-IN-ONE
# CURRY POWDER

MAKES ENOUGH TO FILL A HALF-PINT JAR

Some people think curry powder is a magic wand that you can add to a dish with no other spices, but really, we always use curry powder along with other layers of spices. If you cook your way through the recipes in this book, you'll get a flavor for this. We love whole spices, along with ground spice blends. This medley of spice, however, is special and makes a wonderful rub for vegetables, fish or meat.

4 tablespoons coriander seeds
3 tablespoons cumin seeds
1 tablespoon black peppercorns
seeds from 30 cardamom pods (see Tip)
5 dried bay leaves
3 cinnamon sticks
1 whole nutmeg
2 teaspoons fennel seeds
2 teaspoons cloves
2 teaspoons caraway seeds
2 teaspoons ground ginger

1  Place a skillet over medium heat. Add all the ingredients apart from the ground ginger and dry roast until fragrant and lightly toasted, about 2 minutes. Spread out over a plate to cool and let sit.

2  Once cool, transfer the spices to a spice or coffee grinder or mortar and pestle and grind to a fine powder. Stir the ground ginger into the spice mix, then store in an airtight container and use within 6 months.

TIP

If you don't want to deseed all those cardamom pods, simply toast and grind them whole, along with everything else, and then strain the entire mixture to remove the husks.

# GUNPOWDER SPICE MIX

South India's spice hero, this is the magic bullet for households where not everything is affordable. Sprinkle a little Gunpowder on a dish and it instantly lifts it. This spicy powder is so versatile. It can be sprinkled over dosas (see page 86) and it is awesome stirred into lentils or rice with a little oil or ghee. Try it as a dry dip for idlis and you'll be happy you did.

½ cup idli rice
6 ounces urad dal
2 tablespoons chana dal
7 whole dried Kashmiri chiles
15 dried curry leaves
2 teaspoons asafoetida
1 cinnamon stick
seeds from 3 green cardamom pods
2 teaspoons black peppercorns
1 teaspoon sesame seeds
a pinch of sea salt

1 Set a large skillet over medium heat. Add the idli rice, urad dal, and chana dal and dry-roast for 2–3 minutes or until the mixture turns light brown in color. Transfer to a plate, spread out evenly and let sit to cool.

2 Add the chiles to the same pan and dry-roast for 30 seconds.

3 Remove the chiles from the pan and add to cool with the toasted rice and dal. Mix the dried curry leaves in, spread out the mixture evenly and let sit to cool for 15 minutes.

4 Add the remaining ingredients and grind in a spice or coffee grinder or mortar and pestle to a slightly coarse powder.

5 Store in an airtight container in a cool place for up to 6 months.

## NOTE
You can buy idli rice, urad dal, and chana dal in specialist Indian stores, some larger grocery stores or online.

# MALVANI GARAM MASALA

MAKES ENOUGH TO FILL A HALF-PINT JAR

Garam masala hastens the metabolic system and is very much a staple of Indian cuisine, but every household will have their own recipe, and some will have various different blends of garam masala that they use for different dishes. This one has its roots in the South Konkan region of Maharashtra on the western coast of India where they eat a lot of fish. This particular blend of garam masala spices is, indeed, perfect for seafood dishes, especially mussels and crab. It's also lovely with chicken.

2 tablespoons coriander seeds
2 tablespoons black peppercorns
2 tablespoons fennel seeds
1 tablespoon cloves
1 teaspoon black cumin seeds
4 cinnamon sticks
3 blades of mace
6 bay leaves
seeds from 15 green cardamom pods
seeds from 3 black cardamom pods
2 star anise
4 dried Kashmiri red chiles

1 Place a heavy skillet over medium heat. When hot, add the whole spices and chiles, reduce the heat and dry-roast for 3–5 minutes or until aromatic and lightly toasted. Spread out over a plate and let sit to cool.

2 Once cool, transfer the spices and chiles to a spice or coffee grinder or mortar and pestle and grind to a fine powder. Store in an airtight container in a cool place and use within 6 months.

# KOLHAPURI ROASTED MASALA

This is a rich, unusual masala, as it has roasted onions in the mix. It's very much geared towards red meat and poultry. It's also lovely with game.

¼ cup coriander seeds
½ teaspoon cumin seeds
1 tablespoon dried coconut
½ teaspoon sesame seeds
½ teaspoon black peppercorns
½ cinnamon stick
2 cloves
¼ teaspoon fennel seeds
2 teaspoons canola or olive oil
½ onion, thinly sliced
2 garlic cloves, thinly sliced
¼ cup freshly chopped cilantro leaves
2–3 tablespoons chile powder, to taste
a pinch of sea salt

1  Place a large skillet over medium heat. When hot, dry-roast the coriander seeds, cumin seeds, coconut, sesame seeds, black peppercorns, cinnamon stick, cloves and fennel seeds until fragrant and lightly toasted—about 2 minutes. Spread out over a plate to cool and let sit.

2  Return the skillet to the heat, add the oil and, when hot, fry the onion with a pinch of salt until golden and a little crisp. Add the garlic and fresh cilantro and cook, stirring, for 5 minutes until everything is nicely golden and crisp. Let sit to cool completely.

3  Transfer the spices and the onion mixture to a spice or coffee grinder or mortar and pestle and grind to a fine powder. Stir the chile powder into the spice mix, then store in an airtight container in the refrigerator for up to 2 weeks.

# FENNEL AND CLOVE CHILE SAUCE

MAKES ABOUT 1 CUP

This is a wonderful chile sauce created by Nirmal. The fennel seeds and cloves give it a rounded flavor, and a hint of sweetness among the spices.

4 ounces fresh red chiles, deseeded
½ pound tomatoes, finely chopped
2 teaspoon dried chile flakes
2 tablespoons fennel seeds
2 cloves
1 teaspoons yellow mustard seeds
⅓ cup red wine vinegar
1 teaspoon superfine sugar
2 teaspoons sea salt

1  Place the red chiles in a spice or coffee grinder or mortar and pestle and grind to a paste.

2  Place a skillet over medium heat, add the tomatoes and cook for about 10–15 minutes until broken down and soft. Add the chile paste, chile flakes, fennel seeds, cloves, mustard seeds, red wine vinegar, sugar, and salt and simmer for 5 minutes. Pass through a strainer to make a smooth sauce.

3  Pour into a sterilized botted and cork tightly. Store in the fridge. You can eat it right away, but it tastes best if you wait for 1 week to let the flavors mature. Once opened, use within 2 weeks.

# ANDHRA LAMB PICKLE

Every mother and grandmother in India makes pickles, as it's a way of preserving food, especially when there are no refrigerators. Pickles also add so much flavor to dishes—if you have a bland dish or a food you don't much like, just add pickles and it's suddenly transformed into something palatable.

1 tablespoon turmeric powder
1 tablespoon freshly grated ginger
3 garlic cloves, finely minced
1 pound diced mutton
1 cup canola oil
2 teaspoons chile powder
juice of 5 lemons
sea salt

FOR THE SPICE MIX
½ teaspoon fenugreek seeds
½ teaspoon cumin seeds
½ teaspoon nigella seeds
½ teaspoon coriander seeds

1 In a bowl, mix together the turmeric, ginger, and garlic with a pinch of salt. Massage the flavorings into the mutton and let sit for 30 minutes.

2 Place a skillet over medium heat. When hot, add the fenugreek, cumin, nigella, and coriander seeds and dry-roast until fragrant and lightly toasted—about 2 minutes. Spread out over a plate to cool and let sit.

3 Once cool, transfer the spices to a spice or coffee grinder or mortar and pestle and grind to a fine powder. Let sit.

4 Place a pot over medium heat. Add the mutton and cook in the dry pan for 10 minutes, stirring often, until nicely colored and quite dry. Add the oil to the pot, increase the heat and fry the mutton until the meat turns golden reddish. Add the chile powder and the spice blend you made earlier and cook, stirring, for 2 minutes.

5 Stir in the lemon juice and cook for an additional 2 minutes, then take off the heat and let sit to cool. Transfer to an airtight container and store in the refrigerator until ready to use within 2 weeks. Delicious served alongside a rice dish or with dosas, raita and chutney.

# FISH PICKLE

In India, we make this with king fish, which is very similar to mackerel. It's a sea fish found in the Indian Ocean and it's most popular in southern India, where Nirmal is from. It's an expensive fish and is often served in many fine dining restaurants in India. Here it's used in a quite a thrifty way, as a pickle, which not only preserves it so that it will for keep longer, but also helps stretch the experience of eating it as you'd only have a dollop of the pickle alongside a rice- or lentil-based meal.

1 teaspoon chile powder
½ teaspoon turmeric powder
2 teaspoons freshly grated ginger
2 garlic cloves, finely minced
1 green chile, finely chopped
3 tablespoons freshly chopped cilantro
7 ounces skinless mackerel or king fish fillet, cut into small pieces
3 tablespoons canola oil
1 teaspoon ground fenugreek seeds
3 tablespoon mustard powder
½ teaspoon red chile powder
¼ teaspoon asafoetida
4 teaspoons bottled lemon juice or white wine vinegar
sea salt

1 In a bowl, mix together the chile powder, turmeric, ginger, garlic, green chile, cilantro, and a pinch of sea salt to make a paste. Mix the fish through the paste, ensuring that it's well coated. Marinate for 10 minutes.

2 Set a skillet over high heat. Add 1 tablespoon of the oil. Reduce the heat to medium and fry the marinated fish for about 5 minutes until it's cooked through. Remove from the pan and let sit until cool.

3 Place a clean skillet over medium heat. Add the remaining 2 tablespoons of oil. Once hot, stir in the fenugreek and mustard powder. Cook for 30 seconds, stirring continuously, then add the chile powder and mix well.

4 Add the fried fish pieces and a pinch of salt, then mix the fish through the spices. Cook for 2 minutes, then take off the heat. Stir in the lemon juice or wine and season with salt.

5 It's ready to eat straight away, or can be packed into a sealed jar and stored in the refrigerator for up to a week. Eat hot or cold alongside rice, on toast, in sandwiches or with salad.

# SHRIMP PICKLE

SERVES 4

The tradition of making pickles is one that needs to be preserved. The art is dying, but we're keen to keep it alive. It's the perfect way to lengthen the life of food, but pickles also add so much more texture and flavor to food.

FOR THE FRIED SHRIMP
7 ounces fresh shrimp, shelled and deveined
4 tablespoons canola oil
¼ teaspoon turmeric powder
sea salt

FOR THE TEMPERING SPICES
1 garlic clove, thinly sliced
6 curry leaves (fresh are best if you can get them, but dried are fine)
1 teaspoon yellow mustard seed
¼ teaspoon cumin seeds
8 fenugreek seeds
2 dried kashmiri chiles, broken into two or three pieces

FOR THE PICKLE PASTE
1 tablespoon canola oil
2 tablespoons freshly grated ginger
4 garlic cloves, finely minced
¼ teaspoon turmeric powder
2 teaspoons chile powder
1 teaspoon ground coriander
½ teaspoon garam masala (store-bought, or see page 161)
¼ teaspoon ground cumin (see Tip)
juice of 1 large lemon

1 Set a large skillet over medium–high heat. Add the oil, stir in the shrimps and fry for 2–3 minutes until the shrimps are light pink.

2 Reduce the heat to low. Fold in the turmeric powder and a pinch of salt. Fry for a minute or until the shrimps are nicely coated and golden brown. Take off the heat. Remove the shrimps from the oil with a slotted spoon and let sit.

3 Place the skillet back on the heat, still containing the leftover oil from the shrimps. Add all the tempering spices ingredients and gently fry until the garlic is light brown. Take off the heat and transfer to a plate to cool.

4 Return the skillet to a medium heat. Add the oil for the pickle paste, then stir in the ginger and garlic. Fry for a minute. Add the turmeric powder and fry, stirring, for 30 seconds.

5 Take off the heat and add the remaining ground spices, the tempered spice mixture, and the fried shrimps. Mix well to ensure that everything is well combined. Season with a pinch of sea salt, or to taste.

6 Leave to cool completely, add the lemon juice and mix well. Pack the shrimp pickle into a sterilized jar and seal. Store in the refrigerator for up to a week.

TIP

For maximum flavor, dry-roast whole cumin seeds for 1–2 minutes, or until fragrant, and grind in a spice or coffee grinder or mortar and pestle to make your own roasted ground cumin—the difference in flavor, in comparison to store-bought ground cumin, is remarkable.

# KASHMIRI RADISH AND BEET PICKLE

MAKES 2 X 12 OUNCE JARS

This pickle is a brilliant staple to keep in the refrigerator. It's fantastic with salmon or rice, or any fish or grain-based dish. You can also make a wonderful Indian-style wrap with it together with grilled lamb and a dollop of raita wrapped in a dosa or flatbread.

1½ cups white wine vinegar
2 red beets, peeled, halved, and cut into
   ¾-inch-thick wedges
2 tablespoons sea salt
2 tablespoons sugar
1 tablespoon fennel seeds
2 large daikon radishes, peeled and
   coarsely grated or shaved into long
   ribbons using a vegetable peeler

1  In a large pot, bring the vinegar, beetroot wedges, salt, sugar, fennel seeds, and 1 cup water to the boil. Stir until the salt and sugar are fully dissolved.

2  Remove from the heat and stir in the grated radish. Pack into sterilized jars and seal.

3  Refrigerate for at least 8 hours before serving. The pickle will keep in the refrigerator for up to one month once opened.

# RAW MANGO PICKLE

SERVES 4

Pickles are a wonderful healing food when you're ill. Add them to plain rice or a fairly bland vegetable stew and they're fantastic—both for you and your palate. They're also great as marinades for meat, fish, or paneer.

1 cup canola oil
4 tablespoons yellow mustard seeds, lightly crushed
1 teaspoon fenugreek seeds, crushed
2 tablespoons sea salt
2 teaspoons turmeric powder
2 tablespoons chile powder
1 teaspoon asafoedita
9 ounces unripe mango, cut into 2-inch chunks

1 Set a large pot over a medium heat. Add the oil, then swirl in the crushed mustard and fenugreek seeds and salt. Sauté for 2 minutes.

2 Turn off the heat and add the turmeric. Leave to cool, then add the chile powder. Once cool, stir the diced mango through the mixture to coat in the spices.

3 Pack the pickle into a sterilized jar and store in the refrigerator for at least 24 hours before eating. It will keep for up to a month in the refrigerator.

# APPLE AND DRY FRUIT MURABBA

MAKES 1 PINT

Murabba is a sweet fruit preserve that is popular in India. This version is a recipe handed down from Nirmal's grandmother, who was a cookbook author herself. It's incredibly easy to make and a complete delight to eat at both the breakfast table or with savory rice dishes.

4 medium-sized apples, peeled and cut into 1-inch dice
½ cup golden raisins
½ cup pitted dates, roughly chopped
½ cup dried apricots, halved
¼ teaspoon roasted cinnamon powder
¼ teaspoon ground mace
¼ teaspoon ground ginger
⅛ teaspoon Chinese five spice
2 tablespoons apple cider vinegar
⅔ cup brown sugar
1 tablespoon candied orange peel (or freshly grated zest of 2 oranges)
freshly grated zest of 1 lemon

1  Add the apple, dried fruits, spices, and a tablespoon of the cider vinegar to a heavy-bottomed pot or saucepan along with 5 tablespoons water. Set over medium heat. Pop a lid on and cook for 10–15 minutes, stirring every so often, until the apples are tender. Top up with 1–2 tablespoons of water (or more or less) if the mix starts to look dry.

2  Once the apples are soft, stir in the remaining apple cider vinegar and brown sugar. Simmer over low heat, stirring constantly, until the sugar is dissolved, 2–3 minutes.

3  Fold in the candied orange peel and lemon zest and cook 1 minute longer.

4  The chutney can be eaten right away or pack into a sterilized jar and kept for up to 2 months in the refrigerator. It's delicious alongside a rice pulao or you can even serve it as a compote with yogurt or porridge.

# CAULIFLOWER AND MUSTARD PICKLE

SERVES 6

Nirmal's family have a pickle business in India and this is one of his favorite pickles. I love this one, too—it's beautiful with fish.

¾ cup mustard or canola oil
2 teaspoons fenugreek seeds
3½ ounces crushed yellow mustard seed
2 teaspoons turmeric powder
2 teaspoons asafoetida
9 ounces cauliflower florets (about ½ a head of cauliflower)
½ cup freshly squeezed
2 tablespoons sea salt
1 teaspoon whole yellow mustard seed
1 tablespoon red chile powder

1  In a large saucepan, heat ½ cup of the oil over medium heat, then add the fenugreek seeds and crushed mustard seeds and stir well. Fold in half the turmeric and half the asafoetida. Take off the heat and immediately transfer the mixture to a food processor or blender straight away, so that you don't burn the seeds. Blend to make a paste.

2  Apply the mustard paste to the cauliflower florets. Add the lemon juice and salt.

3  Heat the remaining mustard oil in a skillet. Add the whole mustard seeds and fry until they crackle. Fold the remaining asafoetida through. Turn off the heat and add the remaining turmeric and the chile powder. Mix well. Add this mixture to the cauliflower and mix well.

4  Pack into a sterilized jar and seal. Store in the refrigerator for a week to mature before eating. Use within six weeks.

### NOTE

You can buy crushed mustard seeds in Indian markets or online, but you can make your own by simply grinding whole mustard seeds (in a blender, food processor, or mortar and pestle) to a rough powder.

# BHURANI RAITA

This raita is from Hyderabadi cuisine. It combines the pungency of garlic with the aroma of cilantro and the flavor of popular spices. It's super easy to make—but it tastes special and is delicious alongside biriyani and pulao.

2 cups Greek yogurt
½ teaspoon black salt
¼ teaspoon chile powder
2 tablespoons rapeseed or olive oil
5 garlic cloves, finely chopped
2 tablespoons freshly chopped cilantro

1  Combine the yogurt, black salt, and red chile powder in a bowl and whisk well.

2  Set a small pot over medium heat. Add the oil. Once the oil is hot, add the chopped garlic and fry until golden brown. Let sit to cool.

3  Once the fried garlic is cooled, set a little aside for garnish, then add the rest to the yogurt mixture, along with the oil you fried it in. Mix well and serve garnished with the reserved garlic and the cilantro.

# MANGO AND YOGURT DIP
## (PACHADI)

Nirmal's mother makes this and we all go crazy for it. It's brilliant with lamb dishes or served alongside vegetarian pulao.

1 tablespoon coconut oil
½ teaspoon yellow mustard seed
1 teaspoon washed white urad dal
a pinch of dried chile flakes
a pinch of asafoetida
2 sprigs of curry leaves or 14 whole curry leaves
2 shallots or 1 small onion, finely chopped
2 thumbs of fresh turmeric, peeled and grated
2 green chiles, finely chopped
1 large mango, peeled and diced
1¼ cups Greek yogurt
1 tablespoon freshly chopped cilantro to garnish
sea salt

1  Place the coconut oil in a skillet over medium heat. When hot, add the mustard seeds and wait for them to pop, then stir in the urad dal, chile flakes, asafoetida, and curry leaves and sauté until the leaves turn crisp.

2  Add the shallots or onion, fresh turmeric, and green chile and sauté for 2–3 minutes. Stir through the mango and sauté for 3–4 minutes until it breaks down into a soft, jammy paste. Sprinkle in 1 tablespoon water, or more if necessary, and season with a pinch of salt. Take off the heat and let sit to cool.

3  In a bowl, whip the yogurt until smooth. Fold the mango mixture through, cover and chill in the refrigerator until ready to use. Garnish with the freshly chopped cilantro and serve with a rice or a spicy meat dish.

# SPICED PINEAPPLE RAITA

SERVES 4–6

My wife Devina makes this wonderful raita. It's sweet and cooling—the perfect foil to a spicy dish like the Goan Pork (see page 93). It's also lovely with the Etti Masala (see page 76) and a dosa or rice.

2 cups Greek yogurt
1 teaspoon cumin seeds, toasted
4 tablespoons freshly chopped cilantro
1 teaspoon chaat masala
1 green chile, finely chopped
1 teaspoon superfine sugar
a pinch of black salt or sea salt
7 ounces fresh pineapple, cut into ¾-inch chunks

1 In a large bowl, whip the yogurt until smooth and then mix in half the cumin seeds, half the cilantro, and all the chaat masala, chile, and sugar with the salt. Hold back a few pieces of pineapple to garnish and fold the rest through the spicy yogurt.

2 Cover and chill in the refrigerator until ready to serve, then garnish with the remaining pineapple, cumin seeds, and fresh cilantro.

# BOONDI AND PINK PEPPERCORN RAITA

SERVES 8

My mother makes boondi from scratch—they're little fried drops made from chickpea flour. It's a favorite snack in India, especially in my house. With the yogurt, boondi makes for a fun and delicious raita.

1 cup Greek yogurt
½ teaspoon cumin seeds
½ teaspoon crushed pink peppercorns
2 tablespoons fresh cilantro, finely chopped
½ teaspoon superfine sugar
2 pinches of black salt or sea salt
3½ ounces boondi (crispy fried chickpea drops)

1 In a large bowl, whisk the yogurt until smooth.

2 Place a skillet over medium heat, add the cumin seeds and dry roast until fragrant and lightly toasted—about 1 minute.

3 Mix half the roasted cumin seeds, half the crushed pink peppercorns and half the chopped cilantro into the yogurt with the sugar and salt.

4 Fold the boondi through the yogurt—it will seem like a large quantity, but it's supposed to be a thick mixture.

5 Garnish with the remaining cumin seeds, cilantro, and crushed pink peppercorns. Cover and chill until ready to serve.

NOTE

You can buy boondi in specialist Indian grocers or online.
If you can't find them, puffed rice will also work.

# OKRA RAITA WITH POMEGRANATE

This is one of Nirmal's favorite raitas—the salty cooked okra mixed with the sweet, tangy and juicy pomegranate seeds is such a great combo. This one's so nice, you could almost just eat it on its own.

18 medium-sized okra
5 tablespoons canola or sunflower oil, for frying
1¼ cups organic Greek yogurt
½ teaspoon roasted cumin powder (See Tip on page 167)
¼ teaspoon chile powder
1 teaspoon dried pomegranate seeds (optional)
½ teaspoon superfine sugar
2 tablespoons fresh pomegranate seeds
sea salt

1 Wash the okra well and dry with paper towels, then thinly slice, discarding the woody tops.

2 Place a skillet over high heat. Add the oil and, when hot, shallow-fry the okra, reducing the heat a little, for about 8 minutes until golden all over. Remove with a slotted spoon and drain on paper towels.

3 In a bowl, whisk the yogurt until smooth. Add the roasted ground cumin powder, chile powder, and dried pomegranate seeds and mix together with the sugar and a pinch of salt. Hold back a few pieces of okra to garnish and fold the rest through the spicy yogurt.

4 Cover and chill until ready to serve, then garnish with the remaining okra and fresh pomegranate seeds.

# ROASTED EGGPLANT RAITA

I love this raita—it's very similar to my family's famous roasted eggplant bharta. The key is really roasting the eggplant until it's fully tender and then mashing it with a fork.

1 eggplant
1¼ cups Greek yogurt
3 tablespoons mustard or canola oil
1 shallot or ¼ onion, finely diced
1 large tomato, finely diced
1 green chile, finely chopped
6 garlic cloves, finely chopped
1 teaspoon ground cumin
5 tablespoons fresh cilantro, finely chopped
1 lime
sea salt

1 Roast the eggplant over a gas flame on your stovetop for about 15–20 minutes, turning frequently, or in an oven preheated to 425°F for 40 minutes, until the skin is charred all over and the eggplant is tender right the way through (if you cook it in the oven, remember to prick the skin to avoid it bursting). Let sit to cool.

2 In a bowl, whisk the yogurt until smooth. Peel the burnt skin from the eggplant and remove the stem. Finely chop or mash the cooked eggplant flesh and fold into the yogurt.

3 Place a skillet over high heat. When hot, add the oil, turn down the heat and cook the shallot or onion, tomato, chile, and garlic with a pinch of salt until everything is nicely softened—about 10 minutes. Let sit to cool.

4 Fold the onion-tomato mixture through the yogurt with the cumin and half the cilantro. Cover and chill until ready to serve and then finish with a good squeeze of lime juice, mixing it through, and garnish with the remaining cilantro.

# COCONUT CHUTNEY

SERVES 4

This traditional chutney is made with fresh coconut and lentils, subtly spiced with green chiles and tempered with fresh curry leaves, giving a soothing, earthy flavor. It's the perfect accompaniment for South Indian dosas. It's also great with breakfast dishes, like the Chickpea Pancakes (see page 17), or spicier mains like the Goan Pork (see page 93). *Pictured top.*

1½ cups grated fresh coconut (see Note on page 51)
3 tablespoons dry roasted chana dal (see Note)
½ teaspoon cumin seeds
2 green chiles, roughly chopped
1 large garlic clove, peeled
3–4 tablespoons coconut water
¾ tablespoon canola or coconut oil
¼ teaspoon yellow mustard seed
1 dried red chile, finely sliced
¾ teaspoon washed, dried urad dal (see Note)
4 curry leaves (fresh are best if you can get them, but dried are fine)
a pinch of asafoetida
sea salt

1 Place the grated coconut, roasted chana dal, cumin seeds, green chiles, garlic, and coconut water in a blender and blend into a smooth paste. Spoon into a bowl and let sit.

2 Place a skillet over low heat, add the oil and, when hot, fry the mustard seeds, chile, and urad dal for 1–2 minutes. Add the curry leaves and asafoetida and cook for 1 minute more, stirring, until the leaves turn crisp.

3 Pour the tempering mixture over the blended chutney in the bowl. Season with salt, to taste, cover and chill in the refrigerator until ready to serve.

## NOTE

You can buy urad dal and chana dal in specialist Indian stores, some larger supermarkets or online.

# CILANTRO AND MINT CHUTNEY

# TOMATO AND CILANTRO CHUTNEY

SERVES 4

SERVES 4

This is a classic for barbecued meat—or anything grilled. I also love it with grilled eggplants or tossed with roasted vegetables. You can also use a swirl to garnish soups or toss with leftover shreds of lamb and rice for an instant pulao. *Pictured on page 185.*

1 jalapeño or mild green chile, destalked, cut in half
  lengthwise and deseeded
1 ounce fresh mint leaves
1 ounce fresh cilantro
1 tablespoon freshly squeezed lemon juice
2½ teaspoons freshly grated ginger
2–3 tablespoons Greek yogurt
1 teaspoon chaat masala (see page 10)

1 Place the green chile, mint, cilantro, lemon juice, and ginger in a blender and blitz to a smooth paste.

2 In a bowl, whisk 2 tablespoons of the yogurt with the chaat masala and then fold in the blended mixture. Add more yogurt if needed to make a smooth paste.

3 Cover and chill in the refrigerator until ready to use. It will keep for up to 3 days.

My wife loves this—it's one of her favorites. My mom makes it at home all the time. It's really delicious with the Kale and Corn Cakes (see page 18) or with simple grilled or pan-fried fish.

2 large tomatoes, roughly chopped
3½ ounces freshly chopped cilantro
2 garlic cloves, finely chopped
1 green chile
1 teaspoon cumin seeds
1 tablespoon freshly squeezed lime juice
1 teaspoon superfine sugar
sea salt

1 Place the tomatoes, cilantro, garlic, green chile, and cumin seeds in a blender and blend to a fine paste—don't be tempted to add any water.

2 Transfer to a small bowl and season with the lime juice, sugar, and a pinch of salt. Serve alongside any snack or starter. It will keep in the fridge for up to 3 days.

# RESOURCES

We're extremely passionate about all the recipes in this book and are excited for you to experience the dishes we grew up with and love so much. The list below might help you source some of the more unusual ingredients, which may be harder to find in your local supermarket. You can order most things online, but it's also fun to visit a specialist Indian grocer or supermarket, too, if you have the time and opportunity.

BAZAAR SPICES
Multiple locations in Washington, DC
Tel: 202-379-2907
www.bazaarspices.com

CHERIANS INTERNATIONAL GROCERIES
Multiple locations in and around
   Atlanta, GA
Tel: 404-299-0842
www.cherians.com

GROCERYBABU LLC
1090 Springfield Road
Union, NJ 07083
Tel: 908-686-1500
www.grocerybabu.com

HOUSE OF SPICES (INDIA), INC.
127-40 Willets Point Blvd.
Flushing, NY 11368
Tel: 718-507-4600
www.hosindia.com

KALUSTYAN'S
123 Lexington Ave.
New York, NY 10016
Tel: 800-352-3451
www.foodsofnations.com

KEEMAT GROCERS
Multiple Texas locations in and
   around Houston
Tel: 713-781-2892
www.keematgrocers.com

MADRAS GROCERY STORE
18365 NW West Union Road
Portland, OR 97229
Tel: 503-439-8899
www.madrasgrocerystore.com

NEW INDIA BAZAAR
1107 Polk St.
San Francisco, CA 94109
Tel: 415-928-4553
www.newindiabazar.com

PATEL BROTHERS
Multiple locations nationwide
Tel: 630-213-2222
www.patelbros.com

PATEL BROTHERS USA
42-92 Main Street
Flushing, NY 11355
Tel: 718-661-1112
www.patelbrothersusa.com

PENZEYS
Multiple locations nationwide
Tel: 800-741-7787
www.penzeys.com

# INDEX

# ACKNOWLEDGMENTS

Our sincere thanks to all those who have helped to make this happen. Thank you for supporting and encouraging us in creating *Gunpowder*—both the book and the restaurant.

## ADDITIONAL PICTURE CREDITS

Alamy Stock Photo: Julien Garcia/Hemis 174-175b. Getty Images:
Jeremy Horner 63br; Richard l'Anson 62bl, 174al, 175ar; Tom Cockrem
174-175a. iStock: AAGGraphics 62al; guillermo1956 62-63a; OscarEspinosa
62-63b; RNMitra 175br.